PRAISE FOR
BUY LOW, SELL HIGH

"This book is a good overview of business finance. I think it will be very helpful to all non-financial managers and professionals who want to enhance their knowledge of this subject."

Edward M. Cassar

EVP and CFO, LexisNexis Legal & Professional

"Dr Young's book proves once again that there is an intrinsic connection between business finance and marketing. An extremely helpful book for marketers and salespeople who are trying to be more successful at what they do."

Barry J. Silverman

Senior Director of Strategy, Interbrand

"A practical explanation of how finance is used in the daily life of a business. Phil also does a great job of demystifying accrual accounting as well as the key terms and acronyms that we use in our profession."

William M. Spellman, Jr.

COO/CFO, Mohu

"An effective blend of theory and practice. This is the same approach that I like to use in my finance courses, particularly at the MBA level."

Frank Ryan

CFO, Etaluma and Lecturer in Finance, Fowler College of Business, San Diego State University

"Phil is one of the top educators in our Duke CE global faculty network. I'm delighted that he has decided to put all of the material that he has presented over the years in our finance education offerings around the world into a very readable and useful book."

Patricia W. Longshore

Vice President, Strategic Leadership Solutions, Duke Corporate Education

To Hayden, Emerson and Rui, the lights of my life.

Published by
LID Publishing Inc.
31 West 34th Street, Suite 8004,
New York, NY 10001, US

One Adam Street
London
WC2N 6LE
United Kingdom

info@lidpublishing.com
www.lidpublishing.com

A member of:

BPR
Business Publishers Roundtable

www.businesspublishersroundtable.com

© Dr Philip Young, 2017
© LID Publishing Inc, 2017

Printed in the United States

ISBN: 978-0-9969433-7-6

Cover and page design: Caroline Li

DR. PHILIP YOUNG

SELL
BUY
HIGH
LOW

THE SIMPLICITY OF BUSINESS FINANCE

LID

LONDON NEW YORK BOGOTA
MADRID BARCELONA BUENOS AIRES
MEXICO CITY MONTERREY SAN FRANCISCO
SHANGHAI

CONTENTS

CHAPTER 1

INTRODUCTION:
THE IMPORTANCE OF
BUSINESS FINANCE

WHAT IS BUSINESS FINANCE?

Business finance is about understanding how and why a business makes money. In this book, we explain this by first introducing the main elements of a company's financial report. We then use the key items in this report to evaluate the company's financial health. Following this, we go behind the numbers to explain how people throughout the company make an impact on its financial performance. We close by talking about how a company's financial performance relates to its efforts to increase its shareholder value.

For those who have studied finance in an academic setting, this subject may bring back memories of a thick corporate finance textbook, filled with formulas, theories and discussions about mergers and acquisitions, profit and loss statements and shareholder value. But for those who work in the daily operations of a business organization, finance means down-to-earth tasks such as setting budgets, making sure there is enough cash, and meeting specific revenue or profit targets. These are the activities that are behind the numbers presented in a company's annual report. This is all part of business finance.

WHY IS BUSINESS FINANCE IMPORTANT?

I've spent a good part of my career conducting business finance seminars around the world for non-financial people who work in companies of all shapes and sizes. Companies sponsor these seminars for the professional development of their employees. This in itself might indicate that an understanding of business finance is important. But let me elaborate on some compelling reasons why that is so.

1. Business finance is essentially the language of business. No matter what your job or what type of company you work for, it is important for you to at least be aware of the financial dimension of what you do. If you are on a managerial career track it is even more critical. The higher you rise in management, the more involved you will be with financial planning and budgets, and more responsibility will be placed on you and those you manage to meet certain corporate financial targets.

2. For sales and marketing professionals, it is increasingly important to become trusted advisors to clients and large-account customers. Part of gaining this trust is to understand the financial dynamics and challenges facing customers and clients.

3. The ability to communicate well is a vital part of being a good leader. Understanding business finance is central to being able to communicate financial information in a clear and effective way.

4. If you currently have or want to start your own business, then a solid understanding of business finance is essential. There are numerous examples of entrepreneurs with great ideas who did not succeed because of their lack of financial acumen, particularly in the management of their cash flow.

5. As I caution the participants in my seminars, knowledge of business finance does not necessarily help to make you a successful investor in the stock market. However, understanding business finance is a critical part of being an educated investor.

THE SIMPLICITY OF BUSINESS FINANCE

At the start of my seminars (but thankfully, not at the end!), participants have sometimes told me that they never liked to study business finance, because it is 'confusing' or 'mysterious'. Some have said that math anxiety stops them from wanting to get too involved with numbers. All the business finance that the non-financial person needs to know involves basic arithmetic. Most of the terms and concepts involve everyday business situations. So why do people find such an important subject so challenging or unpleasant to learn? In my view, there are three main reasons for this.

First, there are different terms for the same measure. Take the most common measure of making money: net profit. In business finance, we also call it net income or net earnings. Revenue is the amount of money that a company receives or expects to receive for the sale of its goods or services. It is also called sales, net sales, sales revenue and even net sales revenue. Common expressions for net profit and revenue are also 'bottom line' and 'top line', respectively.

Second, acronyms are often used in place of the actual term. Granted, acronyms are often used in every organizational activity. But when an acronym represents a term that is not understood to begin with, it can become quite confusing. I can say that ROE stands for return on equity. However, if you do not know the definition of equity or what 'return' refers to, then you will indeed be confused.

The third and most important reason why non-financial people find business finance so confusing is because accrual accounting is used in the preparation and presentation of company financial reports. Read on to the next chapter to learn more about accrual accounting. But those not familiar with this method will likely find it difficult to understand the difference between net profit and cash flow. And knowing this difference is vital to your understanding of a business's financial performance.

All three obstacles to learning business finance will be dealt with in the next chapter. Once you are clear about the acronyms and terms commonly used in business finance as well as the basics of accrual accounting, you will find the study of this important subject to be much easier and possibly even interesting. This is why I gave this book the subtitle 'The Simplicity of Business Finance.'

BRIEF SUMMARY OF CHAPTERS

As promised, Chapter 2 explains and clarifies key financial terms and acronyms, as well as the accrual method of accounting. Chapter 3 provides a general framework for how a company makes money. Chapter 4 goes into the details of this framework by showing various types of ratios that are commonly used to assess the financial health of a business. Chapter 5 explains the difference between net profit and cash flow and illustrates the importance of cash and cash flow to a business. Chapter 6, which I think is unique among business finance books available today, discusses the important question, "How can my team and I help to improve our company's financial performance?" Finally, Chapter 7 talks about the efforts made by companies to increase their worth for their owners. For publicly traded companies, this is often referred to as the 'creation of shareholder value'.

SPECIAL FEATURES OF THIS BOOK

Each of the chapters that follow begins with three diagnostic questions, with answers appearing at the end of the chapter. They will be a good check on what you have learned in each chapter or perhaps what you might have remembered if you've studied business finance before.

I have also Included in this book a handy table containing a short list of key financial indicators commonly used to assess the financial health of a business. Participants in my seminars tell me they've found it very helpful. I hope you will too.

CHAPTER 7

UNDERSTANDING THE INCOME STATEMTENT AND THE BALANCE SHEET

DIAGNOSTIC QUESTIONS

1. What is the difference between the income statement and the balance sheet?
2. What is EBIT and where would you find it in a company's annual report?
3. What is the difference between the accrual and cash methods of accounting?

INTRODUCTION

We begin our explanation of how and why a company makes money by first learning to read its annual financial report. Companies tell us about their financial performance using three statements: the income statement, the balance sheet (or statement of financial position) and the statement of cash flows.[1] Figure 1 shows a simplified version of the three statements. In this chapter, we will concentrate on the income statement and the balance sheet. We show the cash flow statement here, but for instructional purposes we explain it in Chapter 5. I have found that if learners have a solid understanding of the income statement and the balance sheet and how they relate to each other, then an understanding of the cash flow statement logically follows. Moreover, most of the commonly used terms and acronyms in business finance are from the income statement and balance sheet.

---

[1] There is a fourth statement called the statement of comprehensive income that is not needed for the purposes of this book.

FIGURE 2.1   ANNUAL FINANCIAL REPORT

Balance sheet 12-31-20XX		Income Statement 20XX	Statement of Cash Flows 20XX
Assets	Liabilities+ Equity	Revenue - Cost of Goods Sold	Net Profit + Depreciation ± Non-financial working capital
Current Assets	Current Liabilities	GROSS PROFIT - Expenses	CASH FLOW FROM OPERATIONS
	Long Term Liabilities	OPERATING PROFIT - Interest	± Investing Activities ± Financing Activities
Non-Current Assets	Equity	- Taxes	CHANGE IN CASH POSITION
		NET PROFIT	

STOCKS AND FLOWS

Before we begin to look closely at the income statement and the balance sheet, here are two important concepts you should know. There are essentially two types of financial measures: 'stock' and 'flow'. A stock measure provides financial information for a given *point* in time, while a flow measure gives us financial information over a given *period* of time. For example, the value of your retirement fund is a stock measure. Its value can be seen at the very moment that you go online to check. On the other hand, the amount that you save and put into your retirement fund each month is a flow measure.

In the same way, a company's balance sheet is a stock measure. It shows the financial position of a company at the end of a certain day. In its annual report, this would be the last day of its fiscal year. The fiscal year for most companies coincides with the calendar year. Conversely, the income statement is a flow measure. It only makes sense if we talk about a company's revenue and net profit generated over a certain period of time. In the case of the annual report, the period is obviously one year. Publicly traded companies must also report their revenue and net profit every three months in what is called the 'quarterly earnings report'. Take one guess (just one) whether the cash flow statement is a stock or a flow measure. Most certainly, it is a flow measure.

THE INCOME STATEMENT

Simply put, the income statement shows whether a company has made any money during a given time period. The income statement is also called the profit and loss statement, or P&L. As you can see in Figure 1, the top line of the income statement is revenue and the bottom line is net profit. In between are the company's costs, expenses, interest and taxes. If all the items in-between are less than the revenue, then the company has made a net profit. If not, then the company has made a loss.

Below are brief definitions of all the terms in the income statement. Recall that one of the reasons why I believe business finance can be confusing to the non-financial person is that there are different terms and acronyms for the same measure. I will try as much as possible to use only one term for each measure throughout this book. However, you should be aware that alternative terms are often used. Listed first are the terms I will use, followed by their alternative names.

Revenue (also called sales, net sales, sales revenue, turnover in the UK or simply the 'top line'): Total monetary amount received or expected to be received from customers from the sale of goods or services during a given reporting period. When the term 'net' is used, it means that the company has adjusted its revenue for such factors as promotional discounts and returned items.

Cost of Goods Sold or COGS, (also called cost of sales / COS, cost of services, or cost of revenue): Total cost of the goods or services that were sold during the reporting period. For manufacturers, this would involve the cost of making the products that they shipped. For a retailer, this would involve the wholesale cost of the goods sold to its retail customers. For a provider of services, this would involve the cost involved in delivering the service to a customer. Typically this is made up largely of labour costs.

Expenses (also called operating expenses): All expenses other than the cost of goods sold or services provided. This can be stated on the income statement simply as 'expenses'. Companies often list expenses by category, such as selling, general and administrative expenses (SG&A), and research and development (R&D). Businesses that spend heavily on R&D, such as technology companies, usually show this category of expenses as a separate item. But the point is that R&D is a part of expenses and not cost.

Depreciation: The portion of the original investment in fixed assets (buildings, machinery, equipment, tools, furniture, etc.) that is recorded as a cost or expense during the reporting period. It reflects a reduction in the value of an asset with the passage of time, due to wear and tear or obsolescence. This item is not always shown separately, but instead included as a cost or as an expense. A related term is amortization, which is the depreciation of intangible assets (discussed further in the section on demystifying accrual accounting).

Interest: The amount of interest that a company must pay over the course of a given time period to those who have loaned it money.

Taxes: Total income tax that the company is required to pay to the government during the reporting period.

Net Profit: (Also called net income, NI, net profit after taxes (NPAT), earnings, net earnings, net earnings after taxes (NEAT), or simply the 'bottom line')

Total amount of money that a company has earned during the reporting period after all expenditures have been subtracted from revenue.

Three Levels of Profit on the Income Statement

Notice in Figure 1 that there are three types of profit shown in the Income Statement: Gross Profit, Operating Profit and Net Profit. Gross profit (GP) is revenue minus cost of goods sold. Operating profit (OP) is gross profit minus expenses. Knowing a company's gross and operating profit helps us to analyze the key factors that influence its ability to make its net profit. We will explain this in Chapters 3 and 4. But for now, just be aware of these three different levels of profit. And for operating profit, be aware that other terms and acronyms used for this measure are Operating Income (OI) and Earnings Before Interest and Taxes (EBIT).

THE BALANCE SHEET

The balance sheet is also called the 'statement of financial position'. It shows the value of a company's assets, liabilities and equity at a given point in time. Following are a brief description of major balance sheet items.

Assets (also called Total Assets)
Assets are resources that a company invests in and owns that are used to generate future revenue, profit and cash flow. The following are general categories of assets reported on a company's balance sheet.

Current Assets: These are either cash or components that the company believes will be converted into cash within one year from the day of the statement of the balance sheet. The other major components are: accounts receivable (A/R) and inventory. Accounts receivable is money owed to the company by its customers and inventory refers to goods bought or produced but not yet sold.

Non-current Assets: Investments in resources that tie up a company's cash for more than one year. There are two main types of non-current assets: Fixed (or tangible) and Intangible.

Fixed Assets: Property, Plant and Equipment (PP&E).

Intangible Assets: Software, patents, brand names and other non-physical resources of long-term value to the company.

Goodwill: Goodwill is considered a type of intangible asset but it is usually listed as a separate item on a company's balance sheet. This is the premium that a company pays to buy another company above and beyond the adjusted book value of the acquired company's assets. A more complete definition is beyond the scope of this book. We list it here because it is such an important item on many companies' balance sheets, particularly those that have grown significantly by buying other companies.

For simplicity, in certain examples provided in this book we will use just two general categories of total assets: current and fixed.

Liabilities (also called Total Liabilities)

Liabilities are binding obligations by a company to pay various entities, such as lenders or suppliers, for loans or bills for services or products delivered but not yet paid. Obligations to lenders (also called creditors) is called debt. Debt obligations require interest payments for the money loaned. Obligation to those involved in transactions other than loans is called 'payables'. Because this usually does not involve an interest payment, payables can be referred to as 'non interest-bearing liabilities' (NIBL). Following are general categories of liabilities reported on the balance sheet.

Current Liabilities: These are obligations that the company must satisfy to its creditors within one year of the statement of the balance sheet. Examples of these are accounts payable (money owed to suppliers), wages and salaries payable (money owed to employees) and notes payable (money owed to short-term lenders such as banks).

Long-term Liabilities: These are obligations that the company must satisfy more than a year after the statement of the balance sheet. An example of this is a 10-year bond.

Equity (Also called Total Equity, Shareholders' Equity or Owners' Equity)

The equity reported on a company's balance sheet is the book value of the owner's investment in the company. It represents the amount of money invested in the company when the shares of stock were originally issued, plus the total accumulated amount of net profit that the company has earned, minus dividends. Book value can probably be best understood when compared to market value. The market value is based on the value of the equity shares trading in the stock market. This is also called 'market capitalization'. Equity is perhaps the most challenging term for non-financial people to understand so we will explain this concept in different ways as we go along in the book. But let's keep it simple for now and think of equity in terms of the following general categories.

Capital Stock (also called common stock, shares issued, shareholder stock, and shareholders' capital): This is the value of the shares of stock when first issued to the general public.

Retained Profit (also called retained income, retained earnings or reinvested earnings): This is the total amount of net profit that the company has earned each year minus what it has paid out in dividends, accumulated in its balance sheet starting from the time the company was established. Because of this, 'accumulated' is sometimes used with this this measure (e.g., 'accumulated retained profit').

Treasury Stock: This is the accumulated amount of money that the company has spent to repurchase outstanding shares of stock owned by the general public. It is shown as a negative amount on the balance sheet, because this activity reduces the value of shareholders' equity.

WHY THE BALANCE SHEET BALANCES

Early on in the semester, every new student in accounting is introduced to 'the accounting equation'. This says that:

$$ASSETS = LIABILITIES + EQUITY$$
$$OR$$
$$A = L + E$$

A complete textbook explanation for why they must be equal (why the balance sheet balances) is beyond the scope of this book. But here are three simplified reasons why the balance sheet balances. First, the right side of the equation represents the sources of a company's funds from suppliers, creditors, and owners. The left side represents the uses of these funds (investment in current and non-current assets). So, the balance sheet balances because the sources of a company's funds equal their uses. Second, the right side of the equation represents the claims on the value of the assets by the people who provided the funds to buy the assets. Thus, the claims by these providers of funds cannot be greater in value than the assets themselves. By the same token, these claims would not be less than the value of these assets, because this would be irrational. Finally, suppose we turn the accounting equation around and express equity as assets minus liabilities. Note the following:.

$$\text{IF: } A = L + E$$
$$\text{THEN: } E = A - L$$

Looked at in this way, we see that a company's equity value is actually the value of what is left if we subtracted the value of the liabilities from the value of its assets. If this is the case, is it then possible for a company to have 'negative equity?' Indeed this would be the case if the company's liabilities were greater than the value of its assets. This would of course be a very troubling situation for a company and not be sustainable for very long!

Check your understanding of the balance by doing the exercise on the following page.

Balance Sheet Exercise: Construct a balance sheet based on the numbers below. Check your work by making sure the balance sheet 'balances'.

Machinery	$20	Money Owed to Suppliers	$15	Shares Issued	$25
Expansion of Manufacturing Facilities	$50	Money Owed to Bond Holders	$30	Wages Owed to Employees	$10
Retained Profit	$20	Money Owed by Customers to the Firm	$15	Money in the Firm's Checking Account	$5
		Computer Servers	$10		

BALANCE SHEET EXERCISE.: WORKSHEET

ASSETS		LIABILITIES AND EQUITY	
Current Assets		**Current Liabilities**	
_____	$___	_____	$___
_____	$___	_____	$___
Fixed Assets		**Long-term Liabilities**	
_____	$___	_____	$___
_____	$___	**Equity**	
_____	$___	_____	$___
		_____	$___
Total	$___	**Total**	$___

BALANCE SHEET EXERCISE: ANSWER

ASSETS		LIABILITIES AND EQUITY	
Current Assets		**Current Liabilities**	
Money in the Firm's Checking Account	$5	Wages owed to Employees	$10
		Money Owed to Suppliers	$15
Money Owed by Customers to the Firm	$15	**Long-term Liabilities**	
		Money Owed to Bond Holders	$30
Fixed Assets			
Machinery	$20	**Equity**	
Computer Servers	$10	Shares Issued	$25
Expansion of Manufacturing Facilities	$50	Retained Profit	$20
Total	**$100**	**Total**	**$100**

DEMYSTIFYING ACCRUAL ACCOUNTING

The branch of accounting that is reponsible for putting the company's numbers together in its annual report for everyone to see is called 'financial accounting'.[2] Financial accountants must follow certain policies and guidelines when preparing the financial statements. One very basic requirement is to use the method of accrual accounting. Here's a simple definition of this method.

Accrual Accounting is the recording of a firm's transactions in the periods when they occur, regardless of whether cash is actually paid or received.

---

[2] Managerial (or cost) accounting is the branch of accounting that gathers and tracks the numbers for internal use; it is for only those within the company to use. In contrast, financial accounting is for external reporting.

In contrast to accrual accounting, 'cash accounting' is the recording of a firm's transactions only when the cash is actually received or paid.

Suppose you are a manufacturer of toothpaste and you just shipped an order for $100,000 worth of product to a wholesale distributor. At the moment the product is shipped, you will be able to count this as a sale. Accountants call this 'revenue recognition.' But most, if not all, business-to-business transactions are not paid immediately. So while you can record the revenue from this sale on your income statement, you do not actually have the cash on hand until the distributor pays you. During the time you are waiting to get paid, the $100,000 will be on your balance sheet as part of 'accounts receivable'.

The same concept could apply to your expenses. Suppose you receive a bill for the services of a marketing consulting firm for $50,000. If you have not paid the company yet, then in effect you would be doing to it what your customer did to you. Its services would be recognized as an expense on your income statement, even though you have not yet paid for them. This amount due would rest on your balance sheet as $50,000 worth of 'accounts payable'. When a company recognizes any expense on its income statement without yet paying for it, accountants use the term 'accrued expense'.

A critical part of accrual accounting is known as the 'matching principle'. It is defined as follows:

> The matching of the costs of producing goods in the same time period in which they were sold. If a good is not yet sold, then its costs are not recorded in the income statement. Instead, they are recorded as inventory on the firm's balance sheet. This is the matching principle.

The matching principle explains why the term *cost of goods sold* (COGS) is used in the income statement, particularly by manufacturing and retail companies. Using the same example of the toothpaste manufacturer, suppose it produces $100,000 worth of toothpaste, but has not yet shipped it to its customer, the wholesale distributor. Consequently, there is no recognized revenue to match with the costs of production. Instead, the cost of these unsold goods is treated as inventory on the company's balance sheet.

DEPRECIATION AND AMORTIZATION

Depreciation is another key concept that can be explained by using the matching principle and accrual accounting. Depreciation is an expenditure that accounts for the use of a company's fixed assets such as plant and equipment. (In financial accounting, property is a non-depreciable asset.) Fixed assets are also called tangible, non-current assets. If the asset is non-current but intangible (for instance, software), then the term is called amortization; same concept, just a different name. Now here is where the matching principle is important. By depreciating only a portion of a fixed asset's total value each year, we are attempting to 'match' the use of that fixed asset with the revenue that it is helping to generate during that year. The same intention applies to the amortization of intangible assets.

There is no perfect way to match up the use of tangible and intangible asset with the revenue associated with their use. But the estimated match up has two parts. Let us use an example involving fixed assets. First, the company must decide on a 'depreciable life' of the fixed asset. There are guidelines that accountants follow regarding this choice. For example, a building can be depreciated over 20 years and certain equipment can be depreciated over 3, 5 or 10 years. Second, a company must decide on the rate at which the depreciation expense will be taken or 'accrued' each year. If the cost of the fixed asset is accrued evenly over its depreciable life, the company is using the 'straight-line' method. If more of the cost of the asset is accrued in the earlier years of its depreciable life and less in its later years, this is called 'accelerated depreciation'. [3]

Figure 2.2 provides a simplified example of how depreciation works and what its impact will be on a company's income statement. For this example, we group costs and expenses into one line item and separate out depreciation. In actual company reports, depreciation and amortization may be included as part of cost of goods sold (the depreciation of a machine used in a factory) or expenses (the depreciation of furniture in a corporate office building).

FIGURE 2.2
DEPRECIATION AND THE MATCHING PRINCIPLE

Depreciation: Per annum amount allocated for the use of a fixed asset that costs $10,000*				
	Yr 1	Yr 2	Yr 3	Yr 4	Yr 5
Revenue	10,000	12,000	15,000	17,500	20,000
Cost and Expenses	8,000	9,000	11,000	13,000	15,000
Depreciation	2,000	2,000	2,000	2,000	2,000
Operating Profit	0	1,000	2,000	2,500	3,000

* Example assumes the use of the "straight-line depreciation method" and also that no further investment in assets is made beyond the first year.

---

[3] Depreciation is a tax-deductible expense. Depreciating faster allows a company to receive greater benefits of this tax shield earlier rather than later.

THE BALANCE SHEET AND NET FIXED ASSETS

When an asset is purchased, it is recorded on a company's balance sheet as part of its 'gross fixed assets'. But as it is depreciated, its remaining accounting value becomes part of what is called 'net fixed assets'. For example, using the same numbers in Figure 2.2 suppose the company bought $10,000 worth of equipment at the beginning of Year 1. This would add $10,000 to the category 'gross fixed assets'. At the end of the year, the company's balance sheet would show an increase in gross fixed assets of $10,000 an increase in 'accumulated depreciation' of $2000 and an increase of net fixed assets of $8,000. Typically, any financial discussion of a company's assets refers to *net fixed* assets.

WHY ARE DEPRECIATION AND AMORTIZATION IMPORTANT FOR NON-FINANCIAL PEOPLE?

As non-financial managers and professionals, you will probably not have to decide on matters such as a fixed asset's depreciation schedule. These types of decisions are left to the company's finance and accounting professionals. But it is important to have a general idea of these concepts for two reasons:

1. Depreciation and amortization could be significant expenses in your operating budget, and if you have financial responsibilities these accrued expenses will affect your operating profit. The higher the investment in fixed or intangible assets, the greater your depreciation and amortization expenses.

2. Depreciation and amortization are important factors in bridging the relationship between accrued profit and cash flow. And, as will be explained in Chapter 5, cash flow is a key measure in the making of operating decisions regarding capital expenditures.

INCOME STATEMENT EXERCISE

Construct an income statement based on the numbers below. Note, some of the items do not belong on this income statement.

Purchase of raw materials used to produce items that were sold	$10	Wages of factory workers that produced goods that were sold during the year	$30
Depreciation of equipment and facilities used in training	$5	Salaries of support staff	$20
Purchase of raw materials used for work in process	$10	Repayment of a loan	$20
Research and development expenditures	$10	Sale of products	$100
Taxes	$5	Interest payment on loans	$4
		Expansion of plant facilities	$50
		Depreciation of equipment used in factory	$10

---

[4] Cost of goods sold cold: Purchase of raw materials (10) Wages of workers(30) and Depreciation of equipment used in factory (10). Expenses: Depreciation of equipment and facilities used in training (5) R&D (10), and Salaries of support staff (20)

INCOME STATEMENT EXERCISE: WORKSHEET

Revenue	$ _____
- Cost of Goods Sold (Includes some depreciation)	$ _____
Gross Profit	$ _____
- Expenses (Includes some depreciation)	$ _____
Operating Profit	$ _____
- Interest	$ _____
- Taxes	$ _____
Net Profit	$

INCOME STATEMENT EXERCISE: ANSWERS[4]

Revenue	$ 100
- Cost of Goods Sold (Includes some depreciation)	$ 50 (10,30,10)
Gross Profit	**$ 50**
- Expenses (Includes some depreciation)	$ 35 (5, 10, 20)
Operating Profit	**$ 15**
- Interest	$ 4
- Taxes	$ 5
Net Profit	**$ 6**

CLARIFYING ALTERNATIVE NAMES AND ACRONYMS

In this chapter, I have tried to provide all the key alternative names and acronyms for each item in the income statement and balance sheet because I know this often confuses the non-financial person. I am also trying to use the same names each time an item or measure is discussed. This is not going to be the case in actual, real-world financial discussions. Consider the following statement:

> 'SHE JUST TOOK OVER THE XYX PRODUCT LINE AND HAS FULL P&L RESPONSIBILITIES. I AM CONFIDENT THAT HER GROUP WILL BE A STRONG CONTRIBUTOR TO THE CORPORATE BOTTOM LINE. BUT LET'S SEE WHAT HAPPENS IN THE NEXT QUARTER'S EARNINGS REPORT.'

In this example, the speaker uses 'P&L' in place of income statement, 'bottom line' instead of net profit, and 'earnings report' instead of quarterly income statement. But you knew that, didn't you?

CONCLUSION

You have just gone through material that in the hands of an accounting professor might take a few weeks to cover! If you are completely new to the field of business finance, I know it has not been easy going. But it will be worth it because we can now start to learn about how and why a company makes money by evaluating the numbers on their income statement and balance sheet.

ANSWERS TO DIAGNOSTIC QUESTIONS:

1. What is the difference between the income statement and the balance sheet? The income statement is a flow measure and shows a company's revenue, costs, expenses, interest, taxes and net profit for a given time period. The balance sheet is a stock measure and shows a company's financial position at a given point in time. One side of the balance sheet shows the value of a company's liabilities and equity (the sources of its funds) and the other shows the value of its assets (where it has invested or used these funds).

2. What is EBIT and where would you find it in a company's annual report? EBIT stands for 'Earnings Before Interest and Taxes'. It is reported in a company's income statement. It is another name for operating profit.

3. What is the difference between accrual and cash methods of accounting? The accrual method of accounting records a company's business transactions in the periods in which they occur, regardless of whether cash is actually paid or received. The cash method records business transactions in the period in which money is actually paid or received.

CHAPTER 3

FINANCIAL DYNAMICS OF A BUSINESS: THE "BIG PICTURE"

DIAGNOSTIC QUESTIONS
1. What is return on equity (ROE) and what does it mean?
2. What is return on assets (ROA) and what does it mean?
3. What are the two major parts of ROA?

INTRODUCTION

Now that you are familiar with the basic elements of a company's income statement and balance sheet, you are ready to learn about how and why a business makes money. The usual measure to determine if a company is making money is net profit. In this chapter we will see that net profit is important, but is actually part of a bigger picture involving the efficient use of a company's assets.

IT TAKES MONEY TO MAKE MONEY

Let's say you wanted to start your own restaurant. You get a special five-year loan from your favorite uncle. You use all of your own savings and convince some friends and other family members to invest in this venture. You find a store front in a great location, fix and furnish it and then open for business. People start to come in to eat. You get rave reviews on social media and you're making a net profit because your revenue is greater than your costs, expenses, interest and taxes. In other words, you're making money! But wait a minute, what about the money that you received to start your business from lenders and investors? How good are you at making money relative to all the money that was required to start and run your business?

Let's assume your revenue for the year was $200,000. After deducting all your costs, expenses, interest and taxes (totaling $190,000), you report a net profit of $10,000. Let's assume further that, at the end of the year, the value of the company's debt and equity are $40,000 each. The money that you owe to your suppliers and employees is $20,000. Figure 3.1 shows how these results would be presented in your company's annual report. The money that you borrowed is shown as a long-term liability. The money that was invested in your business is shown as equity. The money that you owe to your suppliers and employees is shown as current liabilities.

FIGURE 3.1
YOUR RESTAURANT SEEMS TO BE MAKING MONEY

Assets	Liabilities+ Equity	Income Statement (One Year)	
$100,000	**Current $20,000**	Revenue	$200,000
		- Cost of Goods Sold	
	Long Term $40,000	- Expenses	$190,000
		- Interest	
		- Taxes	
	Equity $40,000	NET PROFIT	$10,000

Two common measures of the ability of a company to use money to make money are return on equity (ROE) and return on assets (ROA). The term return on investment (ROI) is sometimes used, but this term can refer to either ROE or ROA so to avoid confusion I will not use it. There is also a measure called return on capital (ROC), but it is a bit more involved so I will discuss it in a later chapter.

ROE and ROA can be computed as follows:

$$ROE = \frac{\text{NET PROFIT}}{\text{EQUITY}}$$

$$ROA = \frac{\text{NET PROFIT}}{\text{TOTAL ASSETS}}$$

Using the numbers in Figure 3.1, we see that

$$ROE = \frac{\$10,000 \text{ (NET PROFIT)}}{\$40,000 \text{ (EQUITY)}} = 25\%$$

$$ROA = \frac{\$10,000 \text{ (NET PROFIT)}}{\$100,000 \text{ (TOTAL ASSETS)}} = 10\%$$

ROE shows the amount of net profit that a company has earned during a year as a percentage of the amount of its equity. ROA shows us the amount of net profit that a company has earned during a year as a percentage of its total assets. Let's look at ROE and ROA in terms of how effective a business is in earning a net profit relative to the money that was provided to start and run the business.

ROE: This is a measure of how effective the business is in using its *owners'* money (i.e., equity) to earn a profit.

ROA: This is a measure of how effective the business is in using everyone's money to earn a profit. In this simple case, "everyone" refers to the lenders (debt), the owners (equity) and the people who are waiting to get paid (current liabilities).

Keep in mind that ROE and ROA *do not* represent actual returns to the owners and lenders. The lenders receive interest payments based on some agreed rate, and the owners would receive dividends if the company chose to make these payments. If the company is publicly traded, its owners would receive a return if the company's share price increases.

ROE, ROA and all the other metrics used by businesses and financial analysts act as indicators of the financial standing of a company. Together they comprise a *scorecard* showing the general financial health of the company. We start with ROE and ROA because they provide a general overview of a company's performance. We'll be getting into the details as we go along.

The evaluation of these and any other financial metric really depends on a number of factors. Have they improved over time? How do they compare with the average of all companies in the stock market, or companies in its industry, particularly its close competitors?

The measure you're probably most familiar with is ROE, because it is often cited in the business media. This indicator of financial performance is especially important for current or potential investors in publicly traded companies, because it focuses on a company's use of the shareholders' money. CEOs know this, so they often use it as a key corporate financial target.

ROA: A BIG PICTURE LOOK AT FINANCIAL PERFORMANCE[1]

Perhaps the most comprehensive measure of the profitability of a business is ROA, because as just stated above it measures how effective the business is in making a net profit using everyone's money. As a teacher, I like to focus on it because it provides a general framework for a company's overall financial performance. Once you understand what ROA is and what causes it to go up or down it will be much easier to understand all the other financial measures, such as those we will cover in the next chapter.

Basically, return on assets is a combination of two key measures: net profit margin and total asset turnover.

Net Profit Margin (also called Return on Sales) measures the ability of a company to earn a net profit relative to the amount of its revenue. The formula for this measure is:

$$\text{NET PROFIT MARGIN} = \frac{\text{NET PROFIT}}{\text{REVENUE}}$$

---

[1] The relationship between ROE, ROA, net profit margin and total asset turnover is what is often called often called "The DuPont Model." It was developed by financial analysts at the DuPont Corporation many years ago.

Total asset turnover is an indicator of a company's ability to utilize all of its assets to generate revenue. Its formula is:

$$\text{TOTAL ASSET TURNOVER} = \frac{\text{REVENUE}}{\text{TOTAL ASSETS}}$$

Turning to the numbers in Figure 1, we see that the company's net profit margin is 5 percent ($10,000/$200,000) and its total asset turnover is 2.0 ($200,00/$100,000). Recall that the company's ROA is 10 percent. So, we can see that return on assets is equal to net profit margin multiplied by total asset turnover. That is:

$$
\begin{array}{ccccc}
\text{RETURN ON} & = & \text{NET PROFIT} & \times & \text{TOTAL ASSET} \\
\text{ASSETS} & & \text{MARGIN} & & \text{TURNOVER} \\
10\% & = & 5\% & \times & 2.0
\end{array}
$$

There is no magic in this relationship. It is simply based on the way we calculate net profit margin and total asset turnover:

$$\frac{\text{NET PROFIT}}{\text{ASSETS}} = \left[\frac{\text{NET PROFIT}}{\cancel{\text{REVENUE}}}\right] \times \left[\frac{\cancel{\text{REVENUE}}}{\text{ASSETS}}\right]$$

But I'd urge you to not get tied up in the math. The fact that ROA is equal to net profit margin multiplied by total asset turnover gives us the **essence of how a company makes money**. Remember that ROA tells us how effective a company is in earning a net profit using everyone's money. This effectiveness in turn is based on a company's ability to earn a net profit relative to its revenue (net profit margin) and its ability to utilize its assets to generate this revenue (total asset turnover).

NET PROFIT MARGIN AND TOTAL ASSET TURNOVER IN DAILY LIFE

Let's put aside the math and think about the net profit margin and total asset turnover in our daily life. Most non-financial people already have a notion of the meaning of net profit margin. Think about the expression, "They make ten cents on a dollar". This means that for every dollar of revenue, the company makes 10 cents of net profit. In other words, this company has a 10% profit margin. That's why another name for net profit margin is return on sales.

You may never have heard of the term total asset turnover, but I am guessing that you already have a general idea of what it means. You've probably heard someone say, "That store is not making much profit but they must be making it up in volume". More volume means more revenue. So, volume is definitely a part of total asset turnover. But total asset turnover also involves assets. Among the key components of a company's total assets are inventory, accounts receivable, and property, plant (such as buildings and factories) and equipment.

The turnover of inventory is something that easily comes to mind. This is what can be seen in a busy market for fresh fish, meats and produce. But what about fixed assets like a building, land or equipment? How do these assets 'turn over'? The confusion that people sometimes have is that fixed assets such as factories, stores and office buildings literally do not 'turn over', so instead of turnover, think about this measure in terms or utilization. It's the same concept, just a different word. Below are some examples of total asset turnover in terms of the utilization of fixed assets.

1. Retail Stores: The utilization of a store location as measured by sales per square foot (or meter).

2. Manufacturing: The utilization of plant capacity as measured by the percentage of the day that the facility is operating, or the volume of output by a factory during a given time period.

3. Hotels: The occupancy rate becomes a critical factor in determining a hotel's total asset turnover.

ROA AS THE FOUNDATION OF A BUSINESS MODEL

In recent years, as we've moved through the digital and internet age, the term 'business model' has become increasingly popular. We talk of 'disruptive' business models such as Uber or Airbnb. You may find a variety of definitions of this term in a web search, but simply stated a business model is 'the way a company makes money'. Using ROA we can say that the way a company makes money is by engaging in activities that affect its profit margin and asset turnover. Here are two extreme examples:

1. A *high profit margin/low asset turnover* business model
2. A *low profit margin/high asset turnover* business model

Suppose we consider two types of retail outlets: a grocery store and a jewelry store. Without looking at any data, how do you think the business models of these two types of stores match up against the two options above? If you think the jewelry store is likely to be #1, you are right! A jewelry store may only sell one bracelet a month but it makes a big profit when it does. A grocery store may only make a small profit margin on each item that it sells, but it sells a lot of these items every day. There are of course many variations between these extreme cases.

Now let us look at another comparison: between companies that make products (manufacturing) and those that sell things (retail).[2]

---

[2] For a detailed listing of ratios for companies classified by industry, sub-industry and size, see the Standard and Poor's resource 'Industry Ratios'.

TABLE 3.1:
AVERAGE MARGIN AND TURNOVER FOR TYPICAL
MANUFACTURING AND RETAIL COMPANIES

	Net Profit Margin	Total Asset Turnover
Manufacturing	5%	1.0
Retail	2%	2.0

Let us apply what you've learned so far with a quick exercise. Using Table 3.1. as a guide, try to match the combination of margin and asset turnover ratios shown in Figure 3.2 with types of business listed below these numbers.

Before checking the answers in the footnote below, you need three correct to pass this test. But notice that you already have the answer to one of them!

Women's specialty shops (e.g., shoe stores and boutique apparel) have an average net profit margin of five percent and a total asset turnover of 1.4.

FIGURE 3.2
MATCH THE INDUSTRY WITH THE APPROPRIATE
PROFIT MARGIN AND ASSET TURNOVER

	A	B	C	D	E	F
Net Profit Margin	5%	10%	4%	2%	5%	16%
Total Asset Turnover	1.0	0.5	1.4	2.2	1.4	0.7

Grocery Stores   _____

Soft Drink Bottlers   _____

Telecommunications Services   _____

Heavy Machinery Manufacturers   _____

Women's Specialty Shops   E

Pharmaceutical Manufacturing   _____

You probably guessed that 'A' was a manufacturing company and 'D' was a grocery store simply by using Table 3.1 as a guide. But how about the other companies? Telecommunications service providers is 'B' and pharmaceutical manufacturers is 'F'. They both have relatively low total asset turnovers and so what distinguishes them from each other is their net profit margin.[3]

Telecom companies have a lot of fixed assets, because of their huge infrastructure of fiber optic cable, cell phone towers and computer

---

[3] Grocery Stores D, Soft Drink Bottlers C, Telecom Companies B, Heavy Machinery Manufacturers A, Pharmaceuticals F.

systems. They also have another type of asset in the form of the licenses that they buy from governments for the rights to use the radio spectrum to carry their wireless services. Pharmaceutical companies also have a lot of assets. Have you ever visited one of their plants? When I did, I was amazed at the size of their operations. From the outside, it looked like a giant chemical plant. On the inside, the equipment and production layout looked more like a high tech manufacturer. It takes a lot of investment in fixed assets to make those little white pills. Further, the non-current assets of the major pharmaceutical companies comprise a considerable amount of goodwill. This is a result of all of the mergers and acquisitions that have taken place in the industry over the past several decades.

The difference in the net profit margin of the telecoms and 'big pharma' stems mainly from the fact that pharmaceutical companies are able to set relatively high prices for their patent-protected drugs. Telecommunications companies are not shielded from competition in this way and so their ability to mark up the prices to cover their costs and expenses are much more limited.

Perhaps the one answer that might have caused some difficulty is 'C', soft-drink bottlers. Have you ever visited a bottling plant? When I did as part of my consulting work for a major beverage company, I was quite surprised at the size of the operations. There are huge containers, high-speed fill lines, trucks, fork lifts, and extruding machines which blow up small plastic bottles to the sizes that are used for the final product. But at the same time, the volume of soft drinks produced every hour is very high. Table 3.2 helps to demonstrate this if we think about it in the following way: 'A' is a manufacturing company that makes the equipment. 'B' is the bottler that buys and uses the equipment. 'C' is the retail company that buys the soft drinks from the bottler and sells it to consumers. So their relative difference in asset turnover of 1.0, 1.4 and 2.2 reflects the relative monetary value of the assets required to generate their respective revenues.

Using ROA as the basis for explaining a company's business model is useful in helping to understand the way companies can disrupt various industries and markets. For example, there are 'asset-light' business models employed by such companies as Uber and Lyft in the transportation industry and Airbnb in the hospitality industry. Not having to own the cars or hotels clearly improves the asset turnover of these companies. On the other side of the ROA equation, companies that provide digital versions of existing products and services for free or very low prices clearly disrupted the profit margins of traditional companies. This has become obvious in such industries as music and publishing.

ROA AND A TALE OF TWO RESTAURANTS

I once heard about the owner of a 'fine dining' Italian restaurant in Midtown Manhattan who each month gave a special bonus to the waiter who served the most coffee and dessert. Why do you think he did this? If you're thinking it's because coffee and dessert are among the higher gross profit margin items on their menu (along with the wine and bottled water), you're absolutely right!

But I also know of the owner of a Chinese restaurant in the New York area whose loyal manager of five years quit and opened up his own Chinese restaurant a few blocks away. (This of course can happen to anyone in any business!) This former employee wanted his Chinese restaurant to be 'special' and so he decided to put fancy desserts and coffee on his menu. "I'm surprised that he didn't learn by working for me that this is not a good thing to do," my owner-acquaintance said to me. "You should never serve coffee and dessert in a Chinese restaurant." Why was he so opposed to this when the owner of an Italian restaurant sought to sell more coffee and dessert by giving his waiters monetary incentives to do so?

When I ask this in my seminars, some participants tell me that it's because tiramisu and cappuccino don't go with Chinese food. But it's not a culinary or cultural thing. Rather, it's all about how each restaurant tries to make money. Or, to put it more formally, it's about their very different 'business models'.

Most fancy Italian restaurants focus on their profit margin. ("Hey, take your time, the table is yours for the night... but please have some dessert, and how about some grappa?"). On the other hand, many Chinese restaurants tend to focus on turnover, so their business model doesn't allow for patrons spending as much time lingering at the table, chatting over coffee and dessert. They would prefer to have a new set of customers come in to buy main meals. So, if you're in a typical Chinese restaurant (in America), please read your fortune cookie and leave!

CONCLUSION

In this chapter, we focused on return on assets (ROA) and its two main components, net profit margin and total asset turnover, to provide an overview of how a company makes money. We used ROA as a key measure, because it is arguably the most comprehensive indicator of how well a company is using money to make money. In the next chapter, we will discuss these measures in much greater detail.

ANSWERS TO DIAGNOSTIC QUESTIONS

1. What is return on equity (ROE) and what does it mean? Return on equity measures the amount of net profit that a company has earned in one year relative to its total equity at the end of the year. It shows how effective the company is in using its owners' money to make a profit.

2. What is return on assets (ROA) and what does it mean? Return on assets measures the amount of net profit that a company has earned in one year relative to the value of all of its assets at the end of the year.. It shows how effective the company is in using everyone's money (creditors and owners) to earn a profit.

3. What are the two major parts of ROA? Net profit margin and total asset turnover.

CHAPTER 1

A DEEPER DIVE
INTO THE NUMBERS

INTRODUCTION

In this chapter, we will evaluate in greater detail the numbers reported in a company's income statement and balance sheet. This method of evaluation is called 'Financial Ratio Analysis'. We actually started using financial ratios in the previous chapter, when I introduced you to return on equity, return on assets, net profit margin and total asset turnover. Each of these measures was composed of ratios between two different items from either the income statement or the balance sheet. For example, net profit margin is the ratio of net profit to revenue. Both items are from the income statement. Total asset turnover is the ratio of revenue (income statement) and total assets (balance sheet).

Almost all of the key ratios that are used to evaluate a company's financial performance can be traced back to ROA. This is the main reason I wanted to help you understand this very important measure in Chapter 3. Figure 4.1 illustrates this point. We have already established that ROA is made up of a combination of net profit margin and total asset turnover. We now also look at the ratios listed in bullets under net profit margin and total asset turnover.

FIGURE 4.1 A DEEPER DIVE INTO ROA

⌐ RETURN ON ASSETS ⌐

NET PROFIT MARGIN
- Gross Profit Margin
- Operating Profit Margin

TOTAL ASSET TURNOVER
- Inventory Turnover
- Accounts Receivable Turnover
- Fixed Asset Turnover
- Non-Cash Asset Turnover

THREE TYPES OF PROFIT MARGIN

Net profit margin is one of three main types of profit margins used in financial ratio analysis. The others are gross profit margin and operating profit margin. We can better understand how the sub-categories of net profit margin shown in Figure 4.1 interact with each other by looking at the income statement. Let's use the Income Statement Exercise in Chapter 2 to illustrate the three basic types of profit margins. This is shown in Figure 4.2 over the page.

FIGURE 4.2 THREE TYPES OF PROFIT MARGINS

		% of Revenue
Revenue	$ 100	
- Cost of Goods Sold (Includes some depreciation)	$ 50	
Gross Profit	**$ 50**	50%
- Expenses (Includes some depreciation)	$ 35	
Operating Profit	**$ 15**	15%
- Interest	$ 4	
- Taxes	$ 5	
Net Profit	**$ 6**	6%

We already know that net profit margin is the ratio of net profit to revenue. In the same way, we determine gross profit margin by looking at the ratio of gross profit to revenue, and operating profit margin as the ratio of operating profit to revenue. In summary:

$$\text{GROSS PROFIT MARGIN} = \frac{\text{GROSS PROFIT}}{\text{REVENUE}}$$

$$\text{OPERATING PROFIT MARGIN} = \frac{\text{OPERATING PROFIT}}{\text{REVENUE}}$$

$$\text{NET PROFIT MARGIN} = \frac{\text{NET PROFIT}}{\text{REVENUE}}$$

Profit ratios are always expressed as percentages. Although it is not a rule, in general, whenever finance people use the term 'margin', they are referring to the ratio (expressed as a percentage). For example, one might say, "We have to be careful about our gross margin falling below 30 percent." Notice also in this expression that financial people sometimes say 'gross margin' as short for 'gross profit margin'.

WHAT THE THREE TYPES OF PROFIT MARGIN TELL US

Gross Profit Margin ("Buy Low and Sell High")

The key factors that affect gross profit margin are: unit cost, unit price and product mix.

> **Unit Price.** If you can increase price without increasing unit cost, then gross profit will increase. A word of caution: an increase in price is often called the 'mark-up'. But you should not confuse the gross profit margin with a mark-up. For example, suppose the wholesale price of a product is $1 and the retail price is $1.50. In other words, the mark-up from the wholesale price to the retail price is 50 percent. That is:

$$(\$1.50 - \$1.00)/ \$1.00 = 50\%$$

But the gross profit margin is actually 33 1/3 percent. That is:

$$(\$1.50 - \$1)/ \$1.50 = 33\ 1/3\%$$

You should be careful about which measure is being discussed. As you can see, the difference in the size of the two percentages is considerable.

Cost of goods sold per unit (also called 'unit cost') A reduction in unit cost while holding price constant will increase the gross profit margin. When we calculate gross profit margin, we can either use the total revenue and the total cost, or the unit revenue (which is the same as price) and the unit cost to obtain the percentage. In both cases, the gross profit margin is the same.

Product Mix. Almost all companies have a mix of products (goods and services) that they provide to their customers. If a company can sell more products with a high gross profit margin, then its overall gross profit margin will increase. For example, the story of the two restaurants told in Chapter 3 talks about an Italian restaurant improving its overall profit margin by selling lots of coffee and dessert, which are both high gross profit margin items.

Operating Profit Margin
("Buy low, sell high, and manage expenses")

Operating profit margin is a reflection of a company's gross profit margin and its ability to manage its expenses. A useful indicator of this ability is the ratio of a company's expenses to its revenue, which can be referred to as the 'expense to revenue ratio' or simply the 'E to R'. Here is its formula:

$$\text{EXPENSE TO REVENUE RATIO} = \frac{\text{EXPENSES}}{\text{REVENUE}}$$

E to R ratios range from 5 percent to as high as 35 percent. To analyze a company's ability to manage its expenses, it is helpful to first know its gross profit margin. Companies with a high gross profit margin can afford to spend more on expenses relative to their revenue and still end up with a respectable operating profit margin. Companies with a low gross profit margin cannot afford to spend much on expenses, because their operating profit margin could soon turn from positive to negative if they are not careful.

The diagram in Figure 4.3 shows a spectrum of possible gross profit margins, from low to high. The benchmark figures used to designate low, medium and high levels are only rough estimates. But what we can say for sure is that the higher the gross profit margin, the more a company can afford to spend on such expenses as marketing, sales, administrative support, and research and development.

Furthermore, financial analysts would generally agree that a gross profit margin above' 50% is 'high' and a gross profit margin below 20 percent is 'low'.

FIGURE 4.3
GROSS PROFIT MARGIN: FROM 'LOW' TO 'HIGH'

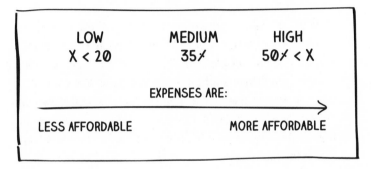

Net Profit Margin (Buy low, sell high, manage expenses, and also manage your interest payments and taxes.)

This is the measure of the overall profit margin of the entire company. Typically, gross profit margin is used to measure the profitability of products and services, while operating profit margin is used to measure the profitability of groups or divisions or perhaps product lines. In this measure of the entire enterprise's profitability, its interest and tax obligations are also taken into account.

WHICH MARGIN ARE WE TALKING ABOUT?

Now that you understand the three types of profit margin, I will caution you that people do not always specify which one they are talking about. For example, consider the following statements; which profit margin are they talking about in each example? Take a moment to think about this before reading the explanations that follow.

1. "One of our main corporate metrics is margin expansion."
   Clarification: At first, one would normally assume the speaker is talking about net profit margin. Typically, net profit margin is used as a measure for the entire company, while operating profit margin is used as a measure for a specific division, product line or sub-group. However, in actual practice, I know that all three types have been singled out by corporate leadership for improvement.

2. "We have to sell higher-margin products in order to improve our overall profitability."
   Clarification: When margin pertains to the types of products being sold, it is most likely referring to gross profit margin.

3. "Our goal is to achieve an EBIT margin of 15 percent by the end of next year."
   Clarification: This is what Americans would call a 'freebie'. As you will recall, EBIT (Earnings Before Interest and Taxes) is the same as operating profit, Therefore, this statement is referring to the operating profit margin.

If you are not sure which of the three profit margins is being discussed, just ask. It is not a silly question, because I have found that, at times, people who use the term are not actually sure themselves which one it is.

TYPES OF TOTAL ASSET TURNOVER

Total asset turnover is the most general measure of asset utilization. It compares a company's revenue with all of its assets. There are also important ratios that use selected sub-categories of total assets. As you know from earlier chapters, there are two basic sub-categories of assets: current and non-current. The first step in our deeper dive into total asset turnover is to look at the turnover of current assets. Let us focus on two types of current assets: accounts receivable and inventory.

Accounts Receivable Turnover (more commonly measured as days outstanding, or DSO)

Accounts receiveable is the amount of money that customers owe to a company at a given point in time. Accounts receivable turnover is computed as:

$$\text{ACCOUNTS RECEIVABLE TURNOVER} = \frac{\text{REVENUE}}{\text{ACCOUNTS RECEIVABLE}}$$

Suppose the company's revenue for the year was $100,000 and at the end of the year it had $25,000 in accounts receivable. Using this information, we see that the accounts receivable turnover is:

$$\text{ACCOUNTS RECEIVABLE TURNOVER} = \frac{\$100,000}{\$25,000} = 4$$

It might be a little confusing to think of the money owed by customers as literally 'turning over', so perhaps the alternative and more commonly used measure, 'days outstanding' (DSO), makes more sense. DSO can be calculated as follows:

$$\text{DAYS OUTSTANDING} = \frac{\text{ACCOUNTS RECEIVABLE}}{(\text{REVENUE}/365)}$$

On average, how long does it take for a company to be paid by its customers? To find the answer we divide $100,000 by 365, This gives us 275.9. We can insert this into the following computation:

$$\text{DAYS OUTSTANDING} = \frac{25,000}{273.9} = 91.3 \text{ DAYS}$$

From the above calculation, we see that this company's customers pay what they owe in an average of 91 days. This is the rough equivalent of the company's accounts receivable 'turning over' four times a year.

Inventory Turnover:

Inventory turnover is the average number of times that a company's stock of goods turns over in a given year. We calculate it as:

$$\text{INVENTORY TURNOVER} = \frac{\text{COST OF GOODS SOLD}}{\text{INVENTORY}}$$

Another way to measure this is to calculate the average number of days that a company's product is part of its inventory before being sold. This is called 'days inventory' and is calculated as:

$$\text{DAYS INVENTORY} = \frac{\text{INVENTORY}}{(\text{COST OF GOODS SOLD} / 365)}$$

Note that the method of calculation for inventory turnover and days inventory is the same as the one we use for accounts receivable turnover and days outstanding. Supoose we assume a company's inventory is $25,000 and its cost of goods sold is $100,000. Then its inventory turnover would be 4.0 and its days inventory would be 91.3. In both cases, a company is tying up some of its cash for about 91 days. But in the first instance it is because its customers have not paid yet and in the second instance, it was because the goods had not yet been sold.

Fixed Asset Turnover

A ratio called "fixed asset turnover" is typically used if we want to focus on the utilization of a company's non-current assets. This shows how effective a company is in utilizing its property, plant and equipment to generate revenue. The fixed asset turnover ratio is mainly used for companies that have a lot of fixed assets such as manufacturers, oil and gas companies, telecommunications companies and electric utilities.

Non-Cash Asset Turnover

By looking at the different sub-categories of current and non-current assts, we have a better undertanding of the magnitude of total asset turnover ratios associated with different types of businesses. Recall in the previous chapter that the total asset turnover ratio of a retail company is about 2.0 and about 1.0 for manufacturing companies. Retail companies do not have as many fixed assets as manufacturing companies. Telecom companies do not have much inventory but they have huge non-current assets in their network infrastructure and their rights to use certain bands of radio spectrum to carry their voice, data, and video services.

Using this same reasoning, we would expect software and digital companies to have high asset turnovers because they do not require as many fixed assets as manufacturing or telecom companies and they don't have any inventory to speak of. But when we look at these types of companies, we find their total asset turnover to be quite low. For example, In Fiscal Year 2016 Microsoft and Alphabet (parent company of Google) had total asset turnover ratios of .44 and .54 respectively.

This apparent contradiction can be explainted by taking a closer look at the balance sheet and income statemets of these types of companies. Typically, companies keep around 10 percent of their assets as cash, cash equivalents, and marketable securities on hand.[3] However, high tech companies, especially software and digital ones, have very high net profit margins of around 20 percent or more. They also do not have to reinvest these profits in a lot of inventory and fixed assets. Therefore, at any one time they can have about 40 or so percent of their total assets as cash, cash equivalents, and marketable securities. Isn't that a nice problem to have? Looking again at Microsoft and Alphabet we see that their total asset turnover for Fiscal Year 2016 without including their cash, cash equivalents, and marketable securities are 1.06 and 1.15 respectively. This is more in line with our expectations.

---

[3] Cash equivalents marketable securities are investments that can be quickly converted into cash with little or no loss in market value (e.g., 30-day treasury bills and bonds close to maturity).

OTHER RATIOS

There are dozens of other financial ratios besides the key ones that we have presented thus far. Those discussed in this book are the direct result of the operating activities of a business. Others that are used include ratios that indicate the abiility of a company to meet its short- and long-term obligations to creditors. Here are a few commonly scrutinized ratios:

Liquidity Ratios

Liquidity is the ease with which an asset can be converted into cash with little or no loss in value. Marketable securities such as government notes are considered so liquid that they are generally included as part of cash, the ultimate 'liquid' asset. Thus they are called 'cash equivalents'. Recall that current assets are resources that tie up a company's funds for less than one year. These are mainly inventories and accounts receivable. Liquidity ratios reflect the ability of a company to meet its short-term obligations, otherwise called 'current liabilities'. The two most commonly used ones are the current ratio and the quick ratio.

$$\text{CURRENT RATIO} = \frac{\text{CURRENT ASSETS}}{\text{CURRENT LIABILITIES}}$$

If this ratio is 2 or more, then it is typically considered 'safe' for a bank to offer a short-term line of credit such as a working capital loan.

$$\text{QUICK RATIO} = \frac{\text{CURRENT ASSETS - INVENTORY}}{\text{CURRENT LIABILITIES}}$$

An argument can be made that inventory is not very liquid because a company might have to sell them off at reduced prices in order to quickly to raise cash. The quick ratio (also called the acid test) adjusts for this possibility. It does not include inventory as part of a company's current assets. If this number is 1.0 or more, then a company is assumed to be safe to lend to on a short-term basis.

Leverage Ratios

Leverage is the use of debt to finance a business. Leverage ratios measure the amount of debt that a company has relative to its equity and other sources of non-interest funds, such as accounts payable. A common measure is:

Once again, the higher this ratio, the greater the leverage.

$$\text{LEVERAGE RATIO} = \frac{\text{TOTAL ASSETS}}{\text{EQUITY}}$$

Leverage is an indicator of financial risk because companies are not obligated to pay dividends but they are required to pay the interest and the principal on their loans.

I will simply point out here that ROA multiplied by the leverage ratio is equal to ROE. Refer to more advanced books in finance to learn about the implications and importance of this relationship.

AVERAGE VS. END-OF-YEAR ASSETS

It is important to note that many of these ratios involve comparing a 'flow measure' with a 'stock measure'. For example, ROA is the ratio between net profit (a flow) and assets (a stock). To adjust for this, we take the average of any stock measure (such as assets) when comparing it to a flow measure. In the case of ROA, we would do the following:

$$\text{RETURN ON AVERAGE ASSETS} = \frac{\text{NET PROFIT IN YEAR 2}}{(\text{TOTAL ASSETS END OF YEAR 1} + \text{TOTAL ASSETS END OF YEAR 2}) / 2}$$

Note that in this formula we use 'average' along with the ratio's name (i.e. return on average asset). For ease of use, I have been using all values on the balance sheet at the end of the year rather than for the average of two years. Either way is correct as long as comparisons are consistent. That is, it would not be accurate to compare the return on assets of one company with the return on average assets of its competitor. The same would apply when comparing a given company's ratios over a number of time periods.

AN IMPORTANT NOTE ON FINANCIAL INSTITUTIONS

By now it might have occurred to you that we have not provided any examples involving financial institutions, such as banks and insurance companies. After all, what better examples of making money are there than companies whose very product is money. This omission is mainly for the ease of explaining concepts. There are many parallels between financial and non-financial businesses. A clothing store buys a product wholesale and sells it retail. A bank buys money wholesale (i.e. pays interest on deposits and money that it borrows) and sells it retail (i.e. charges interest on its loans). The difference between a bank's borrowing and lending interest rate is called the interest rate spread. In effect, this is like the bank's gross profit. Take a guess what is among the highest gross profit products for a bank. That's right: fees!

USING RATIOS TO EVALUATE THE FINANCIAL HEALTH OF A COMPANY

Now that we understand these ratios, how do we use them to evaluate a company's financial performance? When you look at a number, is it good or bad and how much so? The simple answer is, 'that depends'. It depends on the industry that the company is in. It depends on its business model. It depends on the ratios of its competitors. Relative comparisons might be based on the following:

1. Performance over time.
2. Comparison to competitors.
3. Comparison to industry average.
4. Comparison to company targets.

Evaluating the financial health of a business is the subject of Chapter 6.

APPLYING YOUR KNOWLEDE WITH ACTUAL FIGURES

As with learning any new language, the language of finance requires practice in actual, everyday situations. I've provided many simple examples in this book, but there is nothing like trying out what you've learned on real company data. There are many free and paid sites on the internet that provide the data that you need to practice. I recommend a useful site called www.stock-analysis-on. net. It presents detailed information on financial statements, ratios and valuations for the top 100 companies on the New York Stock Exchange and the NASDAQ ranked by their total market capitalization. For example, in just a few minutes I was able to create this table of the revenue and key financial ratios of two well-known US-based global companies that have been fierce, direct competitors for many years. They both sell consumer products with iconic global brands. Can you guess who they are?

GUESS WHO?

	2016	
Revenue (millioins)	$41,863	$62,799
Rev. Growth	-.55%	-.004
Gross Profit Margin	60.7%	55.1%
Operating Profit Margin	20.6%	15.6%
Net Profit Margin	15.9%	10.1%
Total Asset Turnover	.48	.85
Return on Assets	7.48%	8.54%
Return on Equity	28.3%	57.04%
Free Cash Flow (millions)	$6,534	$7,364

Need a further hint? They're both fast-moving consumer goods companies that make and sell carbonated soft drinks. Okay, A is Coca-Cola and B is Pepsi-Cola.

Notice that Pepsi's revenue is much more than Coke's. Also notice that both companies' revenues fell slightly between 2015 and 2016. You'll see that both have high gross profit margins, as expected, but Coke's is 5.6 percentage points higher than Pepsi's. Note that Coke's total asset turnover is considerably lower than Pepsi's.

What explains these differences? I'll leave it to you to ponder. But with just the basics of business finance that you have learned so far, you can go beyond, 'Which one tastes better?'

SUMMARY

Now that you've taken a deeper dive into financial ratios, I hope you're not regreting the fact that you even got into the water! It's time to move on to cash flow to complete your understanding on how to evaluate a company's finanical performance.

ANSWERS TO DIAGNOSTIC QUESTIONS:

1. What is the difference between gross profit margin and net profit margin? Gross profit margin does not consider a company's expenses. Operating profit margin does. That is:

Gross profit margin = (revenue – costs)/revenue
Operating profit margin = (revenue – costs – **expenses**)/revenue

2. Which of the two ratios directly affects the value of a company's assets: days outstanding (DSO) or gross profit margin?

Days Outstanding is the answer. Recall that accounts receivable is classified as a current asset on a company's balance sheet. So the speed at which customers pay their bills (as measured by the number of days it takes them to pay or 'days outstanding') affects the monetary value of a company's accounts receivable at any point in time. Gross profit margin measures a company's gross profit relative to its revenue.

3. Why is gross profit margin such an important indicator of financial performance?

Gross profit margin indicates the amount of leeway that a company has to spend money on such expense items as R&D, sales and marketing, customer support and administrative support. This is particularly important for companies in the manufacturing, retail and services sectors. Software and digital companies generally have very high gross profit margins to begin with, so they are less concerned with this measure, unless adverse changes occur in their business or they are unable to properly manage their expenses.

CHAPTER 5

CASH IS KING: THE IMPORTANCE OF CASH FLOW

In this chapter we present the third of the three key statements in a company's financial report: The Cash Flow Statement. In so doing, we will explain the difference between net profit and cash flow. Cash flow is so important in business finance that I'm sure you've heard the expression 'Cash is king'. This chapter explains why this old saying is so true.

CONVERTING NET PROFIT INTO CASH FLOW

Net profit and cash flow are related but not the same. This is because net profit is calculated using accrual accounting. Therefore, we need to make adjustments to a company's net profit (or loss) in order to determine its cash flow. Suppose someone asked you to calculate a company's net profit by first constructing its income statement. This would look like the left side of the figure oppposite.

FIGURE 5.1
ADJUSTING THE INCOME STATEMENT
TO DETERMINE CASH FLOW

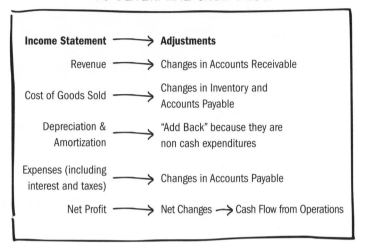

Income Statement ⟶ **Adjustments**

Revenue ⟶ Changes in Accounts Receivable

Cost of Goods Sold ⟶ Changes in Inventory and Accounts Payable

Depreciation & Amortization ⟶ "Add Back" because they are non cash expenditures

Expenses (including interest and taxes) ⟶ Changes in Accounts Payable

Net Profit ⟶ Net Changes ⟶ Cash Flow from Operations

But remember that the amount of revenue may not actually be in cash, because certain customers may not have paid yet. Thus, an adjustment has to be made for the changes in the company's accounts receivable. (See the right side of Figure 5.1.) The income statement records cost of goods sold. What about the cost of goods *unsold*? This goes on the company's balance sheet as inventory.

So in adjusting net profit to determine cash flow, changes in inventory must also be accounted for. The same goes for accrued expenses. Changes in the money owed to its consultants, for example (called 'accounts payable'), must also be accounted for to get the true picture of a company's cash flow. Then there are depreciation and amortization, which we learned in Chapter 2 are non-cash expenditures. To adjust pet profit to cash flow, we have to *add back* the accrued amount of the depreciation taken during the year.

FROM STOCK TO STOCK IS FLOW

Cash flow and accrued profit are both flow measures. That is, they indicate financial performance over a period of time. But many of the adjustments needed to convert accrued profit into cash flow involve items on a company's balance sheet, which is a stock measure. We know that a stock measure shows the company's financial position at a given point in time. We can use stock measures to track flow measures, because a *change* in the value of a stock measure between any two points in time is equal to a flow measure.

Suppose that on the 31st of December a company's accounts receivable was $20,000 and its cash on hand was $1,500. One year later its receivables were $20,500 and its cash on hand was $1,000. Assuming that there were no other changes in its balance sheet, what impact does this increase in accounts receivable have on the firm's cash on hand and its cash flow? The increase in accounts receivable of $500 reduced the company's cash balance by $500. In effect, we say that the increase in the company's accounts receivable (a stock measure) had a negative impact on the company's cash flow (a flow measure). By the same token, a decrease in accounts receivable would increase the company's cash flow, assuming that the other items on the balance sheet do not change.

To test your understanding of this, while all the other factors are held constant, what impact would an increase in accounts payable and a decrease in inventory have on cash flow?

Change on the Balance Sheet	Impact on Cash Flow
1. Increase in accounts receivable	Negative
2. Increase in accounts payable	?
3. Increase in inventory	?

The answers are that an increase in accounts payable would increase cash flow, while an increase in inventory would have a negative impact.

THREE MAIN REASONS WHY CASH FLOWS INTO OR OUT OF A COMPANY

There are three main categories of activity that result in a movement of cash into or out of the company. On the statement of cash flows, they are identified as:

1. NET CASH FROM OPERATING ACTIVITIES.

2. NET CASH FROM INVESTING ACTIVITIES.

3. NET CASH FROM FINANCING ACTIVITIES.

Consider the following:

At the beginning of the year a company has $1,000 of Cash on Hand. During the year the company has net flows of cash in and out through these three activities:

NET CASH FROM OPERATING ACTIVITIES:
+ $3,000.

NET CASH FROM INVESTING ACTIVITIES:
- $2,000.

NET CASH FROM FINANCING ACTIVITIES:
- $500.

How much Cash on Hand does the company have at the end of the year? If you said $1,500, then congratulations. You have grasped the basic concept. The company had a $1,000 'stock' of cash at the beginning of the year. Its net flow from all three activities throughout the year was +500 (3,000 - 2,000 - 500= 500). Therefore, its stock of cash at the end of the year is $1,500 (1,000 + 500 = 1,500).

FIGURE 5.2
CHECKING YOUR UNDERSTANDING
OF THE CASH FLOW STATEMENT[2]

Put "+" (increase in cash) or "-" (decrease in cash)
in the appropriate space below.

Activities	Cash Flow relating to:		
	Operations	Investing	Financing
Sale of product	+	___	___
Sale of office building	___	___	___
Dividend Payment	___	___	___
Buying a new computer	___	___	___
Repayment of a loan	___	___	___

[2] Here are the answers. Sale of office building: + Investing, Dividend payment: - Financing, Buying new computers: - investing, repayment of a loan: - financing

UNDERSTANDING THE CASH FLOW STATEMENT

Upon first glance at any company's cash flow statement, we realize that it might appear to the non-financial person as a dizzying array of line items and numbers. So, to help you, let us outline the essential items.

Cash Flow Statement

Cash on Hand at the Beginning of the Year	
Net Profit	
+ Depreciation and amortization	
+ or - changes in non-financial working capital	
Net Cash from Operating Activities	
- capital expenditures for new fixed assets	
+ cash from sale of assets	
+ or - cash from sale or purchase of short-term investments such as marketable securities	
Net Cash from Investing Activities	
+ new loans	
- repayment of loans	
- dividends paid	
- repurchase of outstanding shares of stock	
+ issuance of new shares of stock	
Cash on Hand at End of the Year	
Net Change in Cash	

Note: This amount is **always** added back because it is a non-cash expenditure

Non-financial working capital refers to a company's current assets and current liabilities. Current financial liabilities such as short-term bank loans are included in the section on financing activities

Cash at beginning of the year minus cash at end of the year

DIFFERENT WAYS TO MEASURE CASH FLOW

If someone says net income, net profit or net earnings, they may be different terms but they all refer to one number: the 'bottom line'.

On the other hand, there are four different ways to measure cash flow. Here they are:

Net cash flow from operations (or just cash flow from operations): This is probably the most commonly used measure. It shows the company's net cash flow over a certain period of time as a result of its daily operations. We know this simply by looking at this line item on the firm's cash flow statement saying "net cash flow from operations".

EBITDA (earnings before interest, taxes, depreciation and amortization): This measure is a common "back of the envelope" measure of cash flow. It calculates operating profit without deducting depreciation and amortization, two major non-cash expenditures that appear on the income statement. But it does not take into account changes in working capital and interest payments and taxes owed.

Free cash flow (FCF): This is:

NET CASH FROM OPERATIONS
- CAPITAL EXPENDITURES
―――――――――――――――――――
= FREE CASH FLOW (FCF)

When financial analysts look at free cash flow, they are seeking an answer to the question, 'How much cash can a company generate in a particular period of time (usually one year) that is free and clear after meeting its basic obligations to pay for its operations and maintain and improve in its physical infrastructure. The idea is that once these obligations are met, then the company is free to use the remaining amount of cash to do such things as pay dividends, pay down debt, repurchase shares of stock or buy another company. As you will see in Chapter 6, FCF can be also used to estimate the value of a company.

Changes in a company's end-of-year cash balance: This measure of cash flow looks at the difference between a company's cash balance at the beginning and at the end of a particular time period. Typically the period is one year, but it can be measured in shorter intervals such as a quarter to quarter or month to month.

If a company's cash balance consistently declines over several time periods, with no prospects of increasing in the near future, this is a serious problem. Some years ago, during the darkest days of the dot-com bust, many tech companies experienced serious cash flow problems. The business press began referring to a 'cash burn rate'. This indicated the time period (usually quarters or months) in which it was feared a company would literally run out of cash!

WORKING CAPITAL

An important way for a company to ensure a strong cash flow is to manage its current assets and current liabilities, also referred to as working capital. Net working capital is calculated as current assets minus current liabilities. When the term 'working capital' is used in everyday financial conversations, it really means net working capital.

The key current assets to consider in the management of working capital are accounts receivable and inventory, and the key current liability is accounts payable. Reducing accounts receivable and inventory while maintaining or even increasing accounts payable helps a company to increase its operating cash flow. When finance people say "our goal is to reduce our working capital", it means that they want to reduce the difference between Current Assets (Accounts Receivable and Inventory) and Current Liabilities (Accounts Payable). Another way of putting this is to say "we want to improve the management of our working capital." In any case, the reduction or improved management of working capital is the essence of that old expression, "Buy low, sell high, collect early and pay late!"

CASH CONVERSION CYCLE

There are a number of ways to monitor how well a company is managing its working capital and hence its operational cash flow. A common measure is called the 'cash conversion cycle'.

This cycle is measured by the length of time on average that it takes for a company to convert cash spent to cash received. More specifically, the formula for this is:

$$\text{CASH CONVERSION CYCLE} = \begin{array}{c} \text{INVENTORY DAYS} \\ + \\ \text{DAYS OUTSTANDING} \\ - \\ \text{ACCOUNTS PAYABLE DAYS} \end{array}$$

We discussed days outstanding and days inventory in the previous chapter. Here is a quick review of accounts payable days.

Accounts payable is the average number of days. This is the average number of days that it takes for a company to pay its suppliers. The longer it takes to pay, the longer the company has to use this cash.

As we see from the formula for the cash conversion cycle, the fewer the days, the greater the company's cash flow from its operations. In short, to manage working capital or operational cash flow, 'Collect early and pay late and sell your products as fast as you can!'

RELATIONSHIP BETWEEN NET PROFIT AND CASH FLOW

Now that you see the relationship between Net Profit and Cash Flow, you can better understand how it is possible for well-established companies (as opposed to start-ups) to lose or make very little money over varying lengths of time (months, quarters and even a few years) and still remain in business. This is possible if the company's cash flow is adequate enough to keep it going in spite of its poor profitability. This situation applies most readily to companies with very high depreciation and amortization charges. They may show an accounting loss but once depreciation and amortization are added back, their net cash flow from operations could be enough for them to continue doing *business*.

On the other hand, you can imagine that it is possible for a company to earn a net profit but still have cash flow problems. Remember that capital investment, high or rising levels of inventory and accounts receivable are not included when calculating a company's accrued profit. Recall that these items are found on the balance sheet and the cash flow statement.

WHEN ARE CASH AND CASH FLOW PARTICULARLY CRITICAL FOR A BUSINESS?

For finance professionals cash is always king. You can keep score with accrued profit, but you actually pay for things with cash. But because all financial results are reported on an accrued basis, the various ratios of profitability (such as ROA, ROE and the different types of profit margins) all represent a standard way of measuring how well a company is doing, particularly if it is well established with above average financial ratios. However, there are certain situations in the life of a company in which cash flow takes absolute precedence over any of the financial ratios in the evaluation of its financial standing. Here they are:

1. *Start-ups*. When a company is just starting out, it is natural for it to require more cash than it generates from its daily operations. Start-ups need a lot of cash for both fixed assets and working capita. In fact start-ups are assumed to have negative cash flows until their revenue reaches a certain level and they also become profitable.

2. *Rapid growth*. Established companies that plan on growing by making major capital investments or by acquiring other companies may need much more cash than normal.

3. *Crisis*. Companies that experience serious cash flow problems due to rapidly decreasing revenue and profit do not necessarily worry about financial ratios per se. They just want to have enough of cash to stay in business. So for companies in this situation, the only measure they look at is cash flow.

4. *High leverage*. There are situations in which a company finds itself with a very high level of debt relative to its equity. This is commonly a result of a 'leveraged buy-out'. In such a case, one company borrows a lot of money in order to buy another one. Once the acquired company becomes part of the acquiring company, the challenge is to have a strong enough cash flow to pay off much or all of this added debt.

Conclusion: Cash flow and net profit are related but not the same, because net profit is computed on the basis of accrual accounting. There are several ways to calculate cash flow. One of the most common is called 'net cash flow from operations'. This can be found on a company's cash flow statement. In a general sense, the cash flow statement represents a combination of a company's income statement and its balance sheet. In any case, now that you are familiar with all three parts of a company's annual report, you are ready to see how people in a company affect the numbers in these financial statements.

ANSWERS TO DIAGNOSTIC QUESTIONS

1. What is the difference between Net Profit and Cash Flow? Net profit is the amount of money calculated on the basis of accrual accounting. Cash flow is the actual money that a company generates after all the adjustments have been made to accrued net profit.

2. How do you measure cash flow? There are many ways. Here are four of the most common measures:

    a. Cash Flow from Operations - This is calculated by adding back depreciation and amortization to net profit (or net loss) and adjusting for changes in non-financial working capital such as changes in accounts payable, accounts receivable and inventory.

    b. Free Cash Flow. This is Cash Flow From Operations minus Capital Expenditures.

    c. EBITDA. This is earnings before (subtracting) interest, taxes, depreciation and amortization. EBIT is calculated soley on the basis of accrual accounting. EBITDA is considered a measure of cash flow, because the non-cash expenditures, depreciation and amortization are *not* considered in the computation.

    d. Changes in the amount of cash on hand between two points in time.

3. What is EBITDA and how does it relate to cash flow? EBITDA stands for earnings before (subtracting) interest, taxes, depreciation and amortization. It is a commonly used way to measure a company's cash flow. In calculating a company's operating profit, EBITDA does not subtract two key non-cash items: deprecition and amortization. However, it does not take into account changes in a company's working capital items such as accounts receivable, accounts payable, and inventory.

CHAPTER 6

YOU MAKE A DIFFERENCE: KEY OPERATIONAL DRIVERS OF FINANCIAL PERFORMANCE

INTRODUCTION

Thus far, we have gone through a lot of terms, acronyms and accounting concepts. Still, the key question remains: How do you and your team make a difference in the company's financial performance? How do you make an impact on the bottom line or on any of the various ratios and numbers that we have discussed in the preceding chapters? To answer these questions, I want you to concentrate on just four terms out of the many presented: Revenue, Assets, Cost and Expense. To emphasize their importance, remember these terms form the acronym RACE. Think of this as a metaphor for the 'race' to business success.

THE KEY DRIVERS OF RACE

On the surface, it would seem obvious what we should do to improve the financial performance of a business through the measures of revenue, assets, costs and expenses. Namely, work to increase revenue, cut costs, manage expenses and invest wisely in assets. In a sense this is true. Below are examples of steps that I have seen taken by many of the companies for which I've consulted. If you are employed by a large company, the list is probably very familiar. 'Lean' and 'Six-Sigma' are performance improvement methodologies that companies use to become more efficient and to enhance the quality of their work.

Here are examples of ways that companies can improve their performance through the effective management of RACE:

Revenue:
1. Innovation and new product development.
2. Improvement of sales efficiency and effectiveness (larger and/or better trained sales force).
3. Marketing (effective market segmentation and targeting).

Assets:
1. Improvement of supply chain management and inventory control.
2. Optimization of capital spending (smart spending on key fixed assets).
3. Faster collection of accounts receivable.

Costs:
1. Better energy management in the factory.
2. Lean manufacturing and six-sigma process improvement training.
3. Outsourcing of selected production processes.

Expenses:

1. Consolidation of a number of relatively small support operations into larger service units of operations ('shared services' and 'centers of excellence').
2. Outsourcing of selected activities that are not core to the business.
3. Lean/Six-Sigma approach to support services (not just in the factory).

Unfortunately, however, the implementatin of any of the above does not guarantee an improvement in financial performance. This is because there are certain trade-offs that must be taken into account. For example, hiring and training more knowledgeable sales people to sell higher-margin products or services seems to make sense. But if the new or rejuvinated sales force is not effective in selling more of the higher-margin products to offset the added expenses, then this would not be a good financial decision. The key to understanding the challenge of improving financial performance through RACE is to keep in mind that, more often than not, there are trade-offs involved. The ROA model that I emphasized in earlier chapters now comes into play to help you understand the challenge of these financial trade-offs.

UNDERSTANDING FINANCIAL TRADE-OFFS USING ROA

ROA, as one of the most comprehensive measures of financial performance, is helpful in illustrating the concept of financial trade-offs. You are well aware that we can calculate ROA by multiplying net profit margin by total asset turnover. (Indeed, I hope that you will never forget this all-important point!) In Table 6.1 we look at three possible combinations of these two ratios that result in an ROA of 10 percent.

TABLE 6.1
THREE COMBINATIONS OF NET PROFIT MARGIN AND TOTAL ASSET TURNOVER WITH THE SAME ROA

	Profit Margin	Asset Turnover	Type of Business
A.	10%	1.0	?
B.	5%	2.0	?
C.	2.5%	4.0	?

Using these numbers as general guidelines, what types of businesses might each combination represent? How about A representing a jewelry store and C representing a grocery store? As noted in a previous example, a jeweler may only sell one bracelet a week (low asset turnover) but it makes a lot of money on each bracelet that it sells (high profit margin). The opposite would hold true for a grocery store.

To further illustrate the concept of a financial trade-off, let me bring back the true story in Chapter 3 about the Chinese and Italian restaurants. In this case, A would represent the 'Italian restaurant' and C would represent the 'Chinese restaurant'.[1] By comparing these two types of restaurants, the margin-turnover trade-off comes to life. The Italian restaurant doesn't mind if patrons spend the evening at the table (lower asset turnover) as long as they order coffee and dessert and other higher margin beverages (higher profit margin). Chinese restaurants may not offer higher-margin food and beverage items, but they offset it with a higher turnover of tables (higher asset turnover). The numbers in Table 6.1 are illustrated in Figure 6.1. Let's now use this figure as a reference point for further dicussion about the margin-turnover trade-off.

The following are some actual business decisions made by companies that I have worked with over the years. The elements of RACE that are affected by these decisions are noted first. I would like you to consider the trade-off between net profit margin (margin) and total asset turnover (turnover) that must be considered in a company's effort to make the right decision.

---

[1] This is an intentionally over-generalized example; there are of course fancy Chinese restaurants and mom & pop neighborhood pizzerias. I've shared this story at seminars in China and Italy and everyone recognizes it as a simple way to visualize how businesses make money.

1. Revenue vs. Expenses

A company decides to hire more sales people with certain knowledge and skills in order to increase sales of higher-margin products and services. Will this increase in expenses be more than offset by an increase in revenue and the sale of higher gross margin products and services?

Impact on ROA: Will a **lower margin** due to increased expenses be more than offset by a **higher turnover** due to increased Revenue as well as the **higher margin** due the sale of higher gross margin products and services?

FIGURE 6.1
THE MARGIN-TURNOVER TRADE-OFF

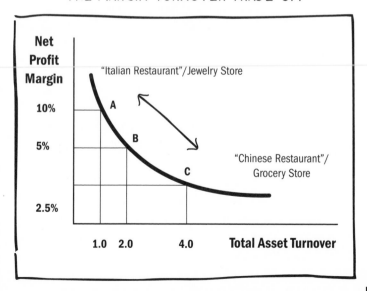

2. Assets vs. Expenses
A major investment is made in new enterprise resource planning (ERP) software in order to reduce the expenses of administrative support.

> Impact on ROA: Will the **lower turnover** due to increased investment in an intangible asset (i.e. software), be more than offset by the **higher margin** due to the decrease in expenses?

3. Revenue vs. Assets
A company decides to make a major investment in new technology with the expectation that it will result in more products that customers will want to buy. Will this investment in new assets pay off in greater revenue (and profit and cash flow) over time?

> Impact on ROA: Will the **lower turnover** due to the increase in assets be more than offset by the higher turnover due to **higher revenue**?

4. Revenue vs. Costs
In an effort to sell more product, sales people offer customers customized products. However, this creates the need for the plant to operationalize different setups and utilize different materials in its production runs. Will the increased revenue generated by catering to special customer requirements offset the higher cost of production?

> Impact on ROA: Will the **higher turnover** due to the increase in revenue be more than offset by the **lower margin** due to the increase in cost?

5. Cost vs. Assets

A company finds that the equipment used in its plant is too old and therefore not as efficient as new equipment. It decides to invest in new equipment. Will the reduction in maintenance expenses and increase in productivity of the new equipment more than offset the increase in capital expenditures over time?

> Impact on ROA: Will the **lower turnover** due to the increase in Assets be more than offset by the **higher margin** due to the reduction in maintenance expenses?

6. Costs vs. Expenses

A company spends a considerable amount of money training its people in lean/six-sigma methodologies in order to become more efficient and to reduce costs associated with production defects.

> Impact on ROA: Will the **lower margin** due to the increased training expenses be more than offset by the **higher margin** due to the reduction in cost of operations?

There are not always obvious answers to what one should do in the face of these trade-offs. It may not be easy, or even possible, to calculate the numerical impact on ROA of these trade-offs between margin and turnover. With the right data, cost-benefit analyses can be conducted. But what is important to know is that there are no guarantees. Business decisions can have positive or negative effects on profitability. As I always say to my seminar particiapants, if only it would be possible to run a business with just a spreadsheet. But simply being aware of the trade-offs involved, and the positive and negative potential of each decision, helps to sharpen your business acumen.

IMPACT ON CASH FLOW

Essentially, the management of cash flow involves items from both the income statement and the balance sheet. But often times finance people prefer to measure the actual outcome in terms of the impact on cash flow rather than on ROA. Lets take a look again at a simplified cash flow statement as an extension of the company's Income Statement. This is shown in Figure 6.2.

FIGURE 6.2
CONNECTING THE INCOME AND
CASH FLOW STATEMENTS

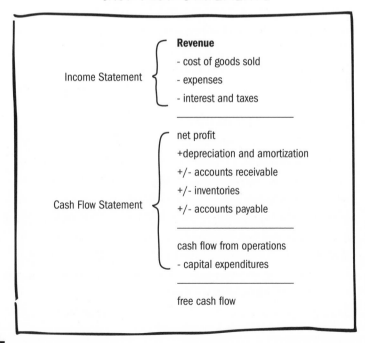

Income Statement
- **Revenue**
- - cost of goods sold
- - expenses
- - interest and taxes

Cash Flow Statement
- net profit
- +depreciation and amortization
- +/- accounts receivable
- +/- inventories
- +/- accounts payable

cash flow from operations
- - capital expenditures

free cash flow

As you can see, most of the items on the cash flow statement can be found on the balance sheet. How do we improve total asset turnover? By managing current and fixed assets. These current and fixed assets are right there on the cash flow statement as changes in accounts receivable, inventories and accounts payable and the amount spent on capital expenditures for the year.

MANAGEMENT OF WORKING CAPITAL

Recall from the previous chapter that working capital comprises current assets and current liabilities. Using working capital as the reference point in the management of cash flow, we can see that in order to enhance cash flow, a company can reduce its accounts receivable and inventories and increase its accounts payable. But just as there were trade-offs when we looked at the operational impact on ROA, there are also trade-offs in the management of working capital.

1. **Inventories: Just in time vs. Just in case**

   Some years ago, Japanese automakers brought to the attention of the business world the importance of 'just-in-time' inventory management. This approach – in which materials or products are acquired or produced more or less in real-time, only as required by marketplace demand – helps to minimize a company's working capital while increasing its cash flow from operations. On the other hand, if the Inventory is too lean, there could be a risk of missing a shipment on the due date, thereby alienating customers and endangering the company's revenue stream.

   Trade-off: Revenue vs. Current Assets

2. **Accounts Receivable: Collect Early vs. Making the Sale**

    "Buy low, sell high, collect early and pay late." We can all recite the mantra, but sometimes sales people offer up easier terms and conditions ('Don't worry about paying right away') as a way of closing a deal. Moreover, a company may find it prudent to allow its biggest and best customers to pay a little later than usual in order to maintain a good relationship.

    Trade-off: Revenue vs. Current Assets

3. **Accounts Payable: Paying Late vs. Continuity of Supply**

    Paying a supplier later rather than sooner is a standard part of managing working capital and enhancing cash flow. But what if suppliers retaliate by shipping slower or not shipping supplies to you at all? To ensure continuity and timeliness of supply, companies may choose to pay their suppliers no later than a certain number of days.

    Trade-off: Production (and Revenue) vs. Current Liabilities

MANAGEMENT OF "CAPEX" IN FIXED ASSETS – ROI AND ITS MEANING

A company's long-term debt and equity is called capital. As much as possible, companies use capital to invest in non-current assets such as property, plant and equipment. When they use it to finance their short-term assets, such as accounts receivable and inventory, it is called working capital. In finance textbooks, a decision to spend money on a multi-year project is called 'capital budgeting'. In industry, it is often called 'making a business case'.

When these decisions are made, a company is making a 'capital investment'. This investment is also called a 'capital expenditure', or 'capex' for short.

WHAT IS A WORTHWHILE INVESTMENT IN CAPITAL?

Suppose you made a capital investment of $300,000, which you believe will generate a cash flow of $100,000 each year for five years. The stream of cash out and cash in would look like this.

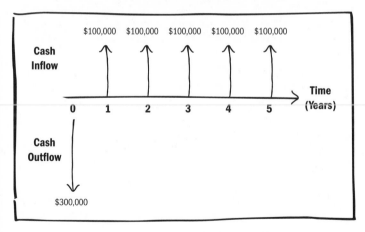

FIGURE 6.3
IS THIS A WORTHWHILE INVESTMENT?

On the surface this would seem to be a worthwhile investment because the total cash in of $500,000 over five years is greater than the cash out of $300,000 in the first year. Another simple way of

justifying this investment is by noting that in three years the investment would pay for itself. The simple pay-back period of this investment is three years. But for finance professionals, this criterion is
not enough because of a factor known as the 'time value of money'.

THE TIME VALUE OF MONEY

The concept of the time value of money means that a given amount
of money received in the future (future value or FV) is worth less
than it would be today (the present value (PV)). Put another way:

> **"A DOLLAR TODAY IS WORTH MORE THAN
> A DOLLAR TOMORROW."**

There are two main reasons for this:[3]

Opportunity Cost: If you receive the money in the future, you
incur an 'opportunity cost' of foregone interest income. In other
words, you have lost the opportunity to invest that money in an
income-earning investment.

Risk: Money received in the future involves risk. Political, mac-
roeconomic or market events could reduce or even destroy the
chances of receiving any money in the future.

---

[3] Inflation is sometimes listed as a third reason, but in most cases the inflation factor
is reflected in interest rates, which represents the magnitude of the opportunity cost.

As savers and investors, we are used to talking about the Future Value of Money. Let's say you put $100 in an investment that gives you an annual rate of return of ten percent. After one year, your investment would be worth $110. More formally, this is how we would calculate this:

Future value (FV) of $100 one year from now, at 10% interest, is calculated as:

$$FV = \$100 \times 1.10$$
$$= \$110$$

Notice that we obtained the $110 by multiplying the original investment of $100 by 1 plus the interest rate or 1.10. To determine what the present value of a future sum of money is, we essentially work backwards by dividing the future value by 1.10.

Present value (PV) of $110 received one year from now is:

$$PV = \frac{\$110}{1.10}$$
$$= \$100$$

When we calculate future value, the percentage that we use in the calculation is called the 'interest rate'. When we find the present value, this same number is called the 'discount rate'.

When we calculate future and present values for a multi-year time period, we have to consider the compounding factor. For example, what is the future value of $100 received 2 years from now, assuming 10 percent interest paid at the end of each year? It is $121 and is calculated as:

FV AT YEAR 1 = $100 X 1.10
             = $110

FV AT YEAR 2 = FV AT YEAR 1 X 1.10
             = $110 X 1,10
             =$121

We can find the answer to the question posed on the next page by extending the logic. As you can see from the question on the next page, the present value of $1,331 becomes less, as it time taken to receive the money increases.

QUESTION

Look at the diagram below and assume a discount rate of 10%. What is the present value of the future stream of $1,331?

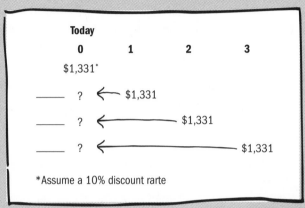

Today

0	1	2	3

$1,331*

——— ? ← $1,331

——— ? ← $1,331

——— ? ← $1,331

*Assume a 10% discount rarte

ANSWER

Money today is worth more than money tomorrow

Money tomorrow is worth less today, and the further out in time the money is received, the less it is worth today

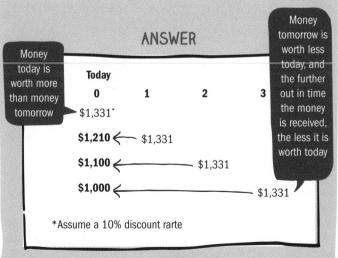

Today

0	1	2	3

$1,331*

$1,210 ← $1,331

$1,100 ← $1,331

$1,000 ← $1,331

*Assume a 10% discount rarte

THE COST OF CAPITAL

From the above discussion, you now see that making a business case for capital investment involves an evaluation of the outflow and inflow of a firm's cash over an extended period of time while taking into account the time value of money. To find the present value of money, a discount rate is required. The discount rate used in capital budgeting analysis is the company's cost of capital. This is a combination of a company's cost of debt and cost of equity.[4] There are two methods of DCF analysis: net present value (NPV) and internal rate of return (IRR).

NPV ANALYSIS

Net present value is the present value of cash flow out minus the present value of cash flow in. If NPV is positive (i.e. greater than zero), then the project is financially sound.

Using the example below, we can assume the company is considering an investment of $300,000 in new equipment today (i.e. time period "0"). Thus, the present value of this is in fact $300,000. We also assume a five-year study period. Over the next five years, it is anticipated that this investment in new equipment will result in

---

[4] The cost of debt is the interest rate that the company pays on its debt. The cost of equity involves a fairly elaborate calculation but it is always higher than the company's interest rate because of the added risks that shareholders take. Unlike debt, equity carries no binding obligation to provide a return to investors either with dividends or the increase in the price of shares.

annual cash inflows of $100,000, because of increased Revenue and cost savings.

Let's further assume that the company's cost of capital is 10 percent. Using this rate and the formula below, we find that the present value of the future inflow of cash over five years is $379,077.

$$\text{Present Value} = \frac{\$100,000}{1.10} + \frac{\$100,000}{(1.10)^2} + \frac{\$100,000}{(1.10)^3} + \frac{\$100,000}{(1.10)^4} + \frac{\$100,000}{(1.10)^5}$$

$$= \$90,909 + \$82,645 + \$75,131 + \$68,301 + \$62,092$$

$$= \$379,078$$

$$\textbf{NPV} = \$379,078 - \$300,000 = \$79,078$$

Clearly we see that NPV is positive. Thus, it would be financially justifiable for the company to invest this money.

IRR ANALYSIS

Internal rate of return is the discount rate that equates the stream of cash inflows with the cash outflow. Once the IRR is computed, it is then compared with the company's cost of capital. If IRR is greater than the company's cost of capital, then the project is financially sound. As it turns out, the IRR for our numerical example is almost 20%, which is clearly greater than the company's cost of capital of 10%.

WHAT METHOD IS BEST?

Both NPV and IRR analysis result in the same conclusion regarding the acceptance or rejection of a capital project.

When NPV > 0
IRR is greater than the cost of capital. (Recommendation: accept the project)

When NPV < 0
IRR is less than the cost of capital. (Recommendation: reject the project)

For theoretical reasons that we will not get into, there are various reasons why finance professors prefer to use NPV over IRR. However, in real life many people prefer to use IRR. In practice, the software used for DCF analysis provides both IRR and NPV.

THE PAY-BACK PERIOD

Sometimes, business decision makers will use a very simple method to decide on whether to make a capital expenditure. This is called the 'pay-back period' and we talked about it in an earlier section.

The pay-back period does not take into account the time value of money. Many small business use it as a quick and easy way to get a general idea of the worthiness of a particular capital project. Indeed, I know of a global technology company whose finance managers will not even consider the NPV or IRR of a project unless it first shows a pay-back of two years or less. The thinking is that technology moves so fast that it is not realistic to rely solely on DCF analysis that involves cash over a longer time period.

THE ROLE OF A NON-FINANCIAL MANAGER IN MAKING A BUSINESS CASE

The task of making a business case is very complex and we have only touched the surface of this important financial analysis methodology. Moreover, in most companies, the finance people are responsible for preparing these business cases for higher levels of management. Huge, multi-million-dollar projects may even be 'pitched' to the CEO and the Board of Directors. Nonetheless, if you are a non-financial manager or professional, you should at least be aware of the basic elements of this type of financial analysis. If you should ever be involved in making a business case, rest assured that a lot of the number crunching will be done by the finance staff. Your main responsibility in the development of the business case would most likely be to provide useful information to estimate the cash outflow and inflow. Non-financial people may also be expected to come up with new ideas on ways that capital expenditures can help to increase the cash flow of the company. Finally, if the business case is approved, it is then the responsibility of non-financial managers and staff to make sure that the investment actually generates the positive NPV stated in the business case.

SUMMARY

The world of business finance may seem complex, with all of its acronyms and ratios and different ways to measure financial success. But from the viewpoint of the vast majority of people who are not in the finance function, it comes down to a very simple set of measures: revenue, assets, cost and expenses. These measures in turn interrelate with each other to form a useful 'big picture' financial indicator called ROA. In closing this chapter, let's think about the everyday work of the people on the front lines of a business and their impact on ROA. These examples are taken directly from my observations in working as an education consultant.

- The help desk professional who goes out of her way to provide a customer with real care and patience to solve a tough problem. (Retaining customers and building recurring revenue.)

- The concierge of a hotel who knows the name of every regular guest. (Building customer loyalty and generating recurring revenue.)

- The engineer who carefully estimated the cost savings that went into the business case for new equipment. (Optimizing the use of capital to help improve asset utilization.)

- The sales manager who made the case for increased training to help his sales team become more effective in account management and solutions selling. (Using Expenses to help generate revenue.)

- The human resources director who realized that the development of an internal capability for recruiting software engineers resulted in a lower churn rate than the company's use of an outside search firm. (Optimizing expenses.)

I could add many more real examples and I'm sure you can add some of your own. In the end, there is no doubt that you and your team do make a difference, no matter how complex the numbers in your annual report may seem.

ANSWERS TO DIAGNOSTIC QUESTIONS:

1. Name at least one way in which a company can improve its gross profit margin and its accounts receivable days outstanding.

   For gross profit margin, it can raise the price, reduce unit costs, sell more products and services with higher gross margins. For days outstanding, it can negotiate more favorable payment terms and improve its billing accuracy.

2. Why is there a potential conflict between 'just-in-time' and 'just-in-case' inventory management?

   Just-in-time inventory control may reduce Inventory levels but leave the company at risk if there is a sudden spike in demand. Just-in-case inventory management may provide a company with a buffer to meet unexpected increases in demand but reduces cash flow from operations.

3. What is one of the most important tasks for non-financial managers and professionals in the preparation of a business case for Capital Spending?

   Financial people rely on the non-financial operations staff to provide reliable data for their NPV and IRR analysis.

CHAPTER 7

CREATING SHAREHOLDER VALUE

DIAGNOSTIC QUESTIONS

1. What is the shareholder value approach to running a business?
2. What is the difference between the market value and the intrinsic value of a company?
3. What is 'profitable growth'?

INTRODUCTION

Over the past 30 or so years, creating or maximizing shareholder value has become an overriding financial goal for many companies, particularly those whose shares are traded in the stock market. This means that, for these publicly traded companies, it is not enough to be financially sound in terms of standard financial indicators such as those that we have presented thus far. The shareholder value approach to managing a business means that whatever metrics are used should evenually translate into greater value for the shareholders in the form of higher stock prices and dividends. In this concluding chapter we explain this approach by defining shareholder value and describing how companies strive to increase value for their shareholders.

WHAT IS THE SHAREHOLDER VALUE APPROACH TO MANAGING A BUSINESS?

There are many groups that have an interest in the financial well-being of a company. These groups are often called 'stakeholders'. They include employees, suppliers, the community in which the company is located, banks, bondholders, the government, and of course the owners. The owners of a public company are generally called shareholders, stockholders or equity owners. The shareholder value approach is one in which the overarching goal of a company is to create value for its owners, the shareholders.

Essentially, the value of a public company is reflected in the price of its shares, which can be traded in the stock market. These shares are called 'shares outstanding'. These shares were first issued to start the company and later more may have been issued to grow the company further. Remember in Chapter 3 the shares that you issued to your friends and family when they invested in your fledgling business? But this was private equity because there was no open market in which your shareholders could resell them to anyone else in the general public. The main goal of the shareholder value approach for publicly traded companies is to strive to increase the value of its shares traded in the stock market. With this in mind, the following are different ways to view the effectiveness of a company's efforts to create shareholder value.

TOTAL MARKET CAPITALIZATION (OR TOTAL MARKET VALUE)

One of the most common measures to show how well a company has done to create value for its owners is called 'total market capitalization', or 'total market value' or 'market cap' for short. This is calculated by multiplying a company's share price by the number of its shares outstanding. That is:

$$\text{TOTAL MARKET CAPITALIZATION} = \text{PRICE PER SHARE} \times \text{NUMBER OF SHARES OUTSTANDING}$$

Look on the internet for lists of 'The World's Most Valuable Companies'. You'll find the usual cast of digital and high tech companies. Depending on the price of oil, you can also expect to find oil and gas companies somewhere in the top 10 on the list.

TOTAL SHAREHOLDER RETURN (TSR)

Besides being rewarded through the rising price of a company's stock that they have purchased, shareholders can also get a return on their investment if and when the company pays them dividends. The combination of dividend payments and stock price appreciation that investors receive is called 'total shareholder return', or TSR. Formally stated:

$$\text{TOTAL SHAREHOLDER RETURN} = \frac{(\text{PRICE}_{END} - \text{PRICE}_{BEGIN}) + D}{\text{PRICE}_{BEGIN}}$$

Where: Price$_{end}$ = share price at end of period
Price$_{begin}$ = share price at beginning of period
D = dividends paid

Suppose you bought stock in a company at the beginning of the year at a price of $100 a share. At the end of the year, the company's stock price rose to $105. The company also paid you $3 in dividends that year. Your TSR for the year would be ($5 + $3)/ $100, or 8 percent.

The Price-Earnings Ratio (P-E or PER) – also called P-E ratio, P-E multiple, and earnings multiple. This is a measure showing the relationship between a company's share price and its earnings per share. That is:

$$\text{P-E RATIO} = \frac{\text{PRICE PER SHARE}}{\text{ANNUAL EARNING PER SHARE}}$$

If last year's earnings per share are used, then this ratio is referred to as the 'trailing P-E ratio'. If the projection of next year's earnings per share are used, then the term 'forward P-E ratio' is used.

Here are some important points to think about when you evaluate the P-E ratio of any company:

1. Is the company's ratio comparable to that of similar types of companies?

2. What is the average P-E ratio in this company's industry? How does the company compare with the industry average? Remember that P-E ratios can differ between different industries.

3. What is the company's growth potential? Generally, companies with higher growth potential have higher P-E ratios.

MARKET-TO-BOOK RATIO (M/B)

Back in Chapter 2, we we noted that the net value of a company's fixed assets on its balance sheet is the cost of the fixed assets minus their accumulated depreciation. We can also call this net value the "book value" of the fixed assets.

Following this line of thought, the book value of a company is determined by subtracting all its liabilities from the book value of all its assets. For example, at the end of a given time period, if a company reports a book value of its assets to be $100 million and its Liabilities to be $80 million, then following the rule that the balance sheet has to balance, the equity is $20 million. This $20 million is the company's 'book value'.

As explained above, the firm's market value is determined by multiplying the number of its shares outstanding by the current share price.

Thus, the market-to-book ratio shows the relationship between a company's total market value and its equity. The formula to compute the market-to-book ratio of a company is:

$$\text{MARKET-TO-BOOK RATIO} = \frac{\text{TOTAL MARKET VALUE}}{\text{TOTAL EQUITY}}$$

If the total market value of a firm's shares of stock is greater than the book value of the owner's equity, the company is in effect creating shareholder value. If a company's market value is greater than its book value, then the market-to-book ratio will be greater than one. There is no specific numerical criterion for evaluating this ratio, other than to say, 'The higher, the better.' Solid performing companies generally have market-to-book ratios of around 3 to 4. Extraordinary companies achieve double-digit market-to-book ratios. But no company can do this indefinitely and eventually even the best of companies settle down to lower-single-digit levels. If the company's market value is less than its book value, this is a strong indication of poor performance in creating value for shareholders.

MARKET VALUE ADDED (MVA)

Market value added is a measure that provides a broader perspective on a company's ability to create value for its shareholders. It compares the company's market capitalization to the cost of the capital that the company has used to support its investment in the business. (Go back to Chapter 5 to review the concept of the cost of capital.)

ENTERPRISE VALUE (EV)

Enterprise value is the value of a company's total market capitalization adjusted for such items as its cash and its debt. It is considered to be the value of the company, for instance, if it were to be taken over by another company.

Suppose a company's market capitalization is $100 million with a debt obligation of $10 million and cash on hand of $5 million. If it were purchased for $100 million, the acquiring company would have to assume its debt of $10 million so taking over the company would really cost it $100 million + $10 million, or $110 million in total. But at the same time the acquiring company has $5 million in cash that it would be able to use. So, the enterprise value(or EV) of this particular company to anyone considering its purchase would be $100 million + 10 million - 5 million, or $105 million in total.[1]

---

[1] There are other details to this computation, such as minority interest.

For purposes of comparison, a company's EV is often expressed as a ratio to other measures of financial performance such as EBIT, revenue and EBITDA. This 'multiples' approach is discussed in the next section.

MEASURING VALUE WITHOUT USING SHARE PRICE

Instrinsic Value of a Company

In an open, competitive market the price of a product is determined by the forces of supply and demand. This is what happens in a stock market. But in this case, 'product' is a share of stock in the company. In addition, financial analysts try to estimate a company's 'intrinsic value', which may not be the same as its current stock price or market value. This approach uses a company's future free cash flow as the basis for valuation. The actual methodology for doing this is very similar to the net present value (NPV) technique explained in Chapter 6.

Instead of finding the net present value of future cash flow relating to a capital project, financial analysts estimate the present value of the future stream of free cash flow of the entire company. This method is often referred to as the 'discounted cash flow' (DCF) method of estimating a company's value. The discount rate that is used to estimate the company's current intrinsic value is its 'cost of capital'.

Details of this approach are beyond the scope of this book, and I have only mentioned it here so that you are aware of this method. For non-financial managers and professionals in a publicly traded company, the key point is to recognize that this analysis uses the future stream of free cash flow to judge a company's intrinsic value. Thus, one reason why a company may be focusing on free cash flow is to influence the analysts' estimate of the intrinsic value of the company. If the intrinsic value of a company's shares is found to be greater than the current stock price, analysts may suggest to investors that its stock is 'undervalued' and therefore considered a good 'buy opportunity'.

But this approach could go in the other direction. In other words, if the analysts' DCF estimation of the company's intrinsic value is less than the stock price, they might conclude that its shares are 'overvalued' and recommend that they either be avoided or sold by those who currently hold shares in this company.

Comparable Multiples

Comparable multiples mean estimating a company's value by comparing it with that of other companies. For example, we have already introduced you to a multiple when we discussed the price-earnings ratio (or P-E Multiple) earlier in this chapter. We can turn this into a 'comparable multiple' analysis by first observing that the average P-E multiple of a company traded on the New York Stock Exchange is about 15. So if a company is trading at a multiple above the average, it could be said that the company is successfully creating value for its owners. The case for this might be even stronger if its P-E ratio is higher than its industry peers. Of course the opposite would hold true if the company's P-E ratio was below the stock market average or the industry average.

As noted above, when a company's EV is compared to other measures, such as revenue, we are in fact using the comparable multiples approach. For example, Company A may have an EV of $100 while Company B has an EV of $50. But suppose Company A's revenue is $50 while Company B's is $20. This implies that Company B is more effective in creating value because its EV is two and a half times its revenue ($50/$20), while Company A's is only twice its revenue ($100/$50).

Because the method of comparable multiples does not involve stock price, it is particularly useful when a company is not publicly traded and therefore has no market price that can be used in its valuation. Two common multiples that are used to determine the value of a privately held company are the 'revenue multiple' and the 'EBIT multiple'. In other words, suppose a private company wants to either sell itself to another company or wants to go public. How does it dress up for the big day? If it knows that companies similar to it are trading at a multiple of three times their revenue, and if it attains revenue of $100 million a year, then it might expect a company interested in buying it to pay up to $300 million for the purchase.

Acquisition Value

The acquisition value is simply the price at which one company is sold to another. In deciding what price to pay for a company, the acquiring company may use such measures as market capitalization, enterprise value, intrinsic value or comparable multiples as estimates of what the company is worth. But in the end, the purchase price that both the seller and buyer agree on becomes the acquisition value.

HOW DOES A COMPANY TRY TO CREATE SHAREHOLDER VALUE?

What can companies do to increase their stock price? This is the crucial question, but one that no one really has THE answer to. There is a saying: 'CEOs of publicly traded companies have two sets of customers – those who buy their products and those who buy their shares of stock'. Since the market value of a company depends on supply and demand, how do CEOs convince investors to buy or hold their companies' shares rather than avoid or sell them?

Many investors rely heavily on the recommendations of stock analysts. Thus, many of the efforts by companies whose shares are traded in the world's leading stock markets are focused on impressing these analysts. Companies know that analysts can judge whether their stocks are worth the investment using any of the metrics we have discussed in this book. So it is up to a company's leadership, in particular the CEO with the help of the CFO, to do the following:

1. Select the target metrics that they believe will best impress the analysts.

2. Set the magnitude of these targets.

3. Hit the numerical targets and highlight this accomplishment in presentations to the analysts, press releases and the annual report.

For example, here is an excerpt from a list of priorities of a manufacturing company that was presented in an investors conference. Noted in parentheses are the financial metrics that I have discussed in this book.

Our Priorities for 2016

- *Achieve higher market average growth* (revenue growth).

- *Grow operating margin to 9% to 10%* (increase in profitability).

- *Maximize Free Cash Flow Generation* (strong cash flow).

- *Further shift the mix of businesses to Consumer [sector]* (product mix and gross profit margin).

Following are other financial metrics that companies consider to be of particular interest to stock analysts.

EARNINGS PER SHARE (EPS)

Earnings per share is one of the most common measures of financial performance for publicly traded companies and a particular favorite among stock brokerage houses. Stock analysts forecast company EPS and the companies themselves often provide guidance to the analysts on what they expect their quarterly and annual EPS to be. Companies that fall short of expected EPS are often hurt by an uptick of selling activity but are helped by a surge of buying activity if their EPS exceeds what is expected.

RETURN ON CAPITAL AND THE COST OF CAPITAL

One of the ways that financial analysts consider a company to be creating value for its owners without using an actual measure of value is to compare its return on capital with its cost of capital. Recall that capital is equity plus debt. The cost of capital is the cost of obtaining this equity and debt. If a company's return on capital is greater than its cost of capital, financial analysts consider a company to be 'creating value'. If it is less, then the company is 'destroying value'.

PROFITABLE GROWTH

Over the past decade, well-established companies have chosen a target called 'profitable growth'. Unlike other metrics presented thus far, this target is not calculated in a specific way like measures such as ROE or 'free cash flow'. ROE is net profit divided by equity, and free cash flow is cash flow from operations minus capital expenditures. But how do you calculate profitable growth? I assure you that you will not find a single, universally agreed upon formula or definition. Based on my experience working with a number of clients who have focused on this measure, I can list at least five different variations. Briefly stated, when a company says its goal is to achieve profitable growth it could mean any one of the following objectives:

- Growth in revenue and growth in earnings per share that is as fast or faster than the top line growth.

- Growth in revenue and expansion in operating profit (i.e. EBIT) margin.

- Growth in revenue and EBITDA margin expansion.

- Growth in revenue and return on capital greater than the company's cost of capital.

- Growth in revenue and return on capital among the top quartile of companies in the industry.

All interpretations have revenue (top line) growth in common, but the second part, showing profitability, differs.

IT'S NOT JUST ABOUT THE NUMBERS

The meaures of the financial health of a business are based on its past performance. When someone buys a share of stock in a company, he or she is investing in a company's future performance. CEOs set financial targets. If their companies hit these targets, they anticipate that they will be rewarded with higher stock prices. But there is no guarantee that this will happen. There may be factors beyond the control of the company, such as downturns in the macro economy, global shifts in trade and foreign exchange, or changes in technology and competition in the markets in which the company competes. In addition, investors look for companies to have what they call a 'growth story'. This is the company's vision and strategy for how it intends to grow its future revenue and profit. They also look at a company's quality of the leadership and general competence (i.e., the 'people factor').

Taken together, then, this is what a company would typically try to do to increase shareholder value:

1. Have a solid, credible growth story with a clear strategy.

2. Execute flawlessly on the strategy.

3. Show excellent and consistent results in all categories of financial metrics, particularly those of most interest to investors, such as ROE, free cash flow, EBIT margin and 'profitable growth'.

4. Have strong and consistent cash flows.

5. Communicate all of the above in a convincing manner to the analysts.

6. And... always hope for the best.

CONCLUDING REMARKS

If you have read through the entire book and reached this point, then I truly hope this will not be the end of your learning journey in business finance. There is so much information available on this subject, in books and on the internet, to help you continue on. It has been my intention to motivate you to learn further by giving you a solid grounding in the fundamentals of business finance in a simple and practical way. For all of you non-financial managers and professionals, particularly in very large business organizations, I hope that you will never again be mystified by or anxious about – or, for that matter, uninterested in – financial presentations and discussions.

ANSWERS TO DIAGNOSTIC QUESTIONS:

1. What is the shareholder value approach to running a business? This is an approach to running a business in which companies try their best to create and maximize value for their owners or shareholders. This approach goes beyond just making money or trying to improve any of the well-known financial ratios.

2. What is the difference between the market value and the intrinsic value of a company? For publicly held companies, the market value is its share price multiplied by its shares outstanding. It is also called its 'market capitalization'. The intrinsic value can be assessed for both public and private companies. It is computed by taking the present value of a company's projected stream of future free cash flow.

3. What is profitable growth? This is a very important financial goal for well-established companies that want to emphasize their attractiveness to the investment community. The idea is that if companies can demonstrate their past and future ability to grow their revenue in a profitable way, investors will continue to buy or hold their shares of stock. There are various ways to demonstrate profitability as we presented in this chapter.

KEY FINANCIAL INDICATORS

1. Top Line Growth	% change in Revenue over time	5-%+ would be nice
2. Bottom Line Growth	% change in Net Profit or Earnings Per Share (EPS)	A growth rate equal to or greater than revenue growth rate shows profitable growth
3. Gross Profit Margin 20%, 35%, 50%+	$$\frac{\text{Gross Profit}}{\text{Revenue}}$$	Buy low, sell high (price, unit cost, product mix)
4. Operating Profit Margin 7%, 10-12%, 20%+	$$\frac{\text{Operating Profit}}{\text{Revenue}}$$	...and manage expenses ('expense to revenue')
5. Net Profit Margin (Return on Sales) 2%, 5%, 10%+	$$\frac{\text{Net Profit}}{\text{Revenue}}$$	...and don't forget interest payments (may depend on leverage) and taxes
6. Total Asset Turnover 0.5, 1.0, 2.0+	$$\frac{\text{Revenue}}{\text{Assets}}$$	Fixed asset utilization, working capital management
7. Return on Assets (ROA) 3%, 5-7%,10%+	$$\frac{\text{Net Profit}}{\text{Assets}}$$	Effective use by management *of everyone's* money
8. Return on Equity (ROE) 10%, 15%, 20%+	$$\frac{\text{Net Profit}}{\text{Equity}}$$	Effective use by management of the *owners'* money
9. Return on Capital (ROC)	$$\frac{\text{Net Operating Profit after Taxes}}{\text{Capital}}$$	Effective use by the management of money they have to pay for
10. Free Cash Flow (FCF)	Cash Flow from Operations Minus Capital Expenditures	Free to use for dividends, paying down debt, buying back stock, buying another business

ABOUT THE AUTHOR

Philip K.Y. Young, Ph.D.

Phil Young is a consultant and former MBA professor with over 30 years of experience in designing and teaching seminars in corporate leadership and personal development in the areas of finance, marketing, and strategy. His primary focus is on courses in finance for non-financial managers and professionals.

His clients include leading global companies in a wide variety of industries including information technology, telecommunications, fast-moving consumer goods, finance, durable goods manufacturing, and pharmaceuticals. He has taught in corporate education programs for his clients in over 30 countries around the world.

He is the co-author of an MBA textbook entitled *Managerial Economics: Economic Tools for Today's Decision Makers* (7th Edition, Pearson). He is also currently an active member of the global faculty network of Duke Corporate Education.

Phil has also developed a business simulation that enables learners to practice using the basic concepts in business finance. It has been used over the years in his seminars and is now offered virtually to colleges and universities as well as to corporate education programs. (beaconsimulation.com). He also writes a finance column that appears regularly in Dialogue magazine (dialoguereview.com).

philyoungconsulting.com